More adoption conversations

Renée Wolfs
Translated by Arthur and Kate Eaton

Published by
British Association for Adoption & Fostering
(BAAF)
Saffron House
6–10 Kirby Street
London EC1N 8TS
www.baaf.org.uk

Charity registration 275689 (England & Wales) and SC039337 (Scotland)

© Renée Wolfs, 2010

British Library Cataloguing in Publication Data
A catalogue record for this book is available from the British Library

ISBN 978 1 905664 96 2

Translated into English by Arthur and Kate Eaton
Project management by Shaila Shah, BAAF
Photograph on cover posed by models by istockphoto.com
Designed by Helen Joubert Designs
Typeset by Fravashi Aga
Printed in Great Britain by T J International
Trade distribution by Turnaround Publisher Services, Unit 3,
Olympia Trading Estate, Coburg Road, London N22 6TZ

BAAF is the leading UK-wide membership organisation for all those concerned
with adoption, fostering and child care issues.

Contents

Acknowledgements

I would like to thank Nelleke Polderman of Basic Trust for her inspiring and helpful advice to me throughout my writing process. Her commitment, expertise and rich experience provided me with the sense that I wasn't in it alone. I would also like to thank Martine Delfos, Joosje Christophersen, Willy de Reus and Corrie Huijbregts for their comments on earlier (Dutch) drafts. With these comments, I was able to approach the text from a different point of view and subsequently make it more profound.

For the English version I would especially like to thank Arthur and Kate Eaton. They really did a wonderful and thorough job in translating my Dutch book into English. I also would like to acknowledge the work done by Paula McDiarmid in editing the English text and for preparing the manuscript. My special thanks go to Shaila Shah: thank you for publishing both of my books! I really hope a lot of adoptive families will benefit from it.

Renée Wolfs

Note about the author

Renée Wolfs is a mother of three children adopted from China. She received her Master's degree in Communication in 1987 and works as a freelance journalist and author. She is also an experienced coach in communication skills and works for a Dutch child helpline. She has written several articles and columns in Dutch adoption magazines.

Her personal involvement in adoption, coupled with her communication expertise and a knowledge of developmental psychology, led Renée to question what exactly children should be told about their adoption story, and at what age. Two books resulted. They were first published in the Netherlands in 2004 and 2008, titled *World Child: Talking to your adopted child* and *The Adoption Dialogue: Conversation techniques for adoptive families with teenagers*, respectively.

The English language edition of *World Child*, titled *Adoption Conversations*, was published in the UK by BAAF in 2008. This in-depth practical guide explores the questions adopted children are likely to ask, up to age 12, with suggestions for helpful explanations and answers.

You can find out more at www.reneewolfs.com.

Your parents are your roots. It is unbearable to be the enemy of one's own roots, because in that way one is the enemy of oneself.
ELSE-MARIE VAN DEN EERENBEEMT

To my father

Introduction

How can I explain the complex feelings of adopted teenagers in plain words? That was my central question when I started writing this book, because it is language that helps us to explain our feelings and get in touch with the world around us. If we can find unambiguous words to represent the complex feelings of adopted children, we will be able to understand better why our children feel afraid, angry or sad. And when we do so, we will automatically become less insecure about their behaviour. Language will build the bridge between us and our children, between our world and theirs.

Ever since I started looking for these "plain words", I have read piles of inspiring professional literature on puberty, parenthood, adoption, loyalty, grief, parenting and communication, among other things. Eventually I had read so much, I could not remember everything any more. I let everything go and set sail on my own acquired knowledge and insight. Here the writing process started. I hope my words will bring you closer to yourself and to the world of your adopted teenager, and that they will help build a bridge between you and your child.

For the chapters on puberty and communication, the books by Martine Delfos (*Ik heb ook wat te vertellen*, 2005a) and Annette

Heffels (*Praten met je puber*, 2006) were especially useful. Both writers convinced me that communication especially is important in this period. I have integrated part of their knowledge into the first, general chapter, which covers (pre)puberty, and also into the final two chapters, which are about communication. Another part of my research was aimed at the specific development of adopted teenagers. Among others, the US book *Beneath the Mask,* by Debbie Riley (2005) was especially helpful in providing me with the tools to disentangle the topics concerning adopted children and their parents from more general subjects on teenagers. Subsequently, and acting on my own discretion, I put into words a number of basic thoughts that adopted children and their parents might have as a result of their history. I have spread these basic thoughts across different chapters throughout the middle of this book, and clarified them to keep them as simple as possible.

Once again (as I did for *Adoption Conversations*), I studied Nelleke Polderman's communication method (2004, 2006), in which sensitive and responsive action is central. I discovered that this interactive method could provide material that is helpful for parents of adopted teenagers. I have integrated Polderman's progressive scheme into Chapter 7. In the two following chapters, I have added a number of solution-directed question techniques from *Constructive Social Work* by Nigel Parton and Patrick O'Byrne (2000) to Delfos and Heffels' (2006) theories of communication, as well as contributing my own knowledge and insights.

Furthermore, the book *De Liefdesladder* by family therapist Else-Marie van den Eerenbeemt provided a lot of inspiration. On nearly every page, she emphasises the importance of the family connection, and of securing this connection. 'Freedom,' she writes, 'is to be found in the acknowledgement of the connection'(Van den Eerenbeemt, 2003, p.47). Without that connection, one denies one's own roots, and therefore one's own identity. The thoughts that Van den Eerenbeemt's has written in *De Liefdesladder* resound in many pages of my book as silent echoes. Lastly, the book *Vertraagde start* (Hoksbergen, 2006), in which 17 adopted children openly discuss their childhood, proved to be very helpful. I have included many of their words and thoughts throughout the book.

As I said at the start of this introduction, language appears to me to be the most important way of reaching your adopted teenager. It is for this reason that I spend more than a third of this book on the dialogue between parent and child. How vulnerable some adopted children feel in their communication with others, and how important it is for us to maintain the dialogue, is clear from the words of the adopted Mirjam Hamoen in *Vertraagde Start* when, at the age of 39, she reflects on her childhood. She writes about the experience of being left at nursery school for the first time:

> I became incredibly alert, my antennas permanently working at their max, eyes in the back of my head and that constant feeling of insecurity, fear, alarm. I ended up on an island, just like my brother. He remained there, while I found ways to get off the island once in a while, when I deemed it necessary. My second nature, which developed rapidly, turned out to be the bridge to contact and communication with the outside world. That bridge became my survival. I could cross from the north side, the pessimistic and withdrawn side, but also from the south side. Exactly where I needed the change. I was also able to haul the bridge up, so no one could access my island, when I wanted to retreat. It's how I created my own security, on my own conditions, according to my own perception and always with the alertness and my antennas.
> (Hoksbergen, 2006, pp.43–44)

Mirjam Hamoen clearly expresses what many adopted children experience in their communication with others. What many of them need is a safe and reliable bridge for them to cross in order to reach the outside world whenever they wish. As a parent, you can build such a bridge by entering the dialogue with your teenager and confronting difficult adoption-related problems together.

What I've learned above all in the process of writing this book is that most adopted teenagers feel different from their peers and that it is important that this "being different" is seen and acknowledged by us as their parents. As has been written many times before, the pain of having been handed over by birth parents is something many carry with them all their lives. That pain surfaces in their relations with others, in their identity, their life history, their appearance and (in many cases) their name.

What I've also learned is that, among the large number of adopted children, every child is different, and that it is important for us parents to realise this. Every child deals differently with his or her adoption. That is why it is essential for us to find out how our child faces his or her own adoption. In that way, it is important for us not to force anything upon our children, not to talk them into problems or unnecessarily bring up their history or original culture. Because however important it seems to most adoptive parents for their children to connect with their history, in the end all children have the right to process and experience their adoption in their own way. It's not up to us to lay the path before them. Some adopted children don't want to grieve or discuss their history (yet) because they are not ready (for whatever reason). They must retain the freedom to go their own way. 'Truth is a pathless land,' as the Indian teacher Krishnamurthi put it. There are as many truths as there are children. When you add your own unique dispositions and biography, and the combination you and your partner form, it ought to be clear that the number of truths is endless. Therefore, I have tried to rid my book of such "truths" as much as possible. What I have particularly tried to emphasise in this book is the fact that there are several extra issues that adopted children and their parents deal with. By providing words for basic thoughts and feelings, we may be able to understand better why our children sometimes feel and act differently than others.

Another important issue that I became aware of while writing is that puberty is not something that parents and children suddenly stumble upon but rather approach together. Puberty is actually a repetition of what has been happening before. If your child got through those earlier stages well, then he or she has a better chance of developing well during puberty and thereafter. Of course, a lot depends on your teenager's predispositions and temperament, adoption history, age of arrival in the family and, last but not least, the degree of basic trust he or she has been able to develop. In that sense, adoptive parents often have a much more complicated task to complete than "normal" parents, and puberty can be a more intense period than usual. For this reason especially, it is important that these children are able to create solid foundations before puberty. I have learned that it's possible for parents to influence that foundation, in part by being aware of several developmental tasks your child should accomplish before puberty and by stimulating these developmental tasks.

For ease of reading, and in order not to favour one sex over the other, I have chosen to use "he" or "she" in alternating chapters.

All unattributed quotations in the book have come from personal conversations with adopted parents or teenagers. Quotations taken from other publications have either come from English-language translated editions, or have been translated by myself for present purposes.

1

Puberty: general developmental characteristics

Puberty
Is just helping parents
To expand their views.
Loesje (an international writers' collective – see www.loesje.org)

Introduction

From their teenage years onwards, children rapidly develop towards adulthood. Body and brain both go through major changes in a short time. Teenagers, for example, gain 30 centimetres in length and 22 kilograms in weight, on average, between the ages of ten and 16. In the brain too, radical changes take place. From approximately their 10th or 11th year, a hectic period begins for many children; a time in which they need lots of privacy, show fierce behaviour and are involved in heavy confrontations with their parents. In this phase, they must learn to cope with their new, adult bodies and their completely new ways of thinking. And, as if this wasn't enough, within this same period they have to obtain autonomy and structure their images of themselves, so that at the end of it they can function on their own in society.

This uncertain time, in which children break free from their parents and bid the safety of childhood farewell, is often experienced by parents as "difficult". It is a period of frequent rows, in which children display unexpected mood swings and sometimes even dangerous behaviour. Scientific research shows that there are arguments almost every day in households with a teenager: on average, there are two rows in every three days, over seemingly trivial matters – and especially between mothers and daughters. Risky behaviour appears somewhat later, from 15/16 years on, with a peak in delinquency at 17 or 18. After that, the chances of risky behaviour rapidly diminish. Between the ages of 14 and 16 particularly, teenagers can display very fierce behaviour, and will sometimes appear to have lost their senses. During this time, their thinking sharpens and in conflicts they can be very blunt. The content of an argument seems less important than the conflict itself. Many parents approach this age with some anxiety and anticipation:

> When my child reached puberty, all of a sudden I was doubting everything. When she was little I was much less affected by this, my role as a parent was probably clearer then. But my girl reached 14, 15, and of course she wanted to go out at night. The first night was fine, she was home on time, the second night she was too, but after that she started coming home later each time. I noticed she was seeing friends whom I did not know well but who had a strong influence on her, and gradually I lost the basic mother–daughter connection. Of course I knew my daughter was growing up, and I should let her go. But how far was I to go in this? Shouldn't I also protect her from dangerous situations? Should I let her go and provide her with the autonomy she was longing for, or was it important for me to stay on top of things, to set her clear rules and provide her with guidelines? Whenever I did set her a rule, the

situation almost inevitably escalated and our dialogue would turn into a nasty argument. Punishment and prohibition were useless by that time; she wouldn't listen and would go her own way. When I tried to give her advice sometimes she would become hysterical even, yelling at me that she was perfectly able to think for herself. Nothing was self-evident any more, all parenting rules became blurred. I hadn't a clue about my position or how to change things.

Even though adolescence is often experienced as a turbulent period filled with conflict, and a time in which parenthood changes drastically, it is also gripping and exciting. It is a period when the child's brain grows explosively, and endless numbers of synapses are established within it. As a consequence, teenagers have the feeling they understand everything. They start to participate in discussions and substantiate their arguments, and they stubbornly defend their ideals and beliefs. In fact, there isn't any other time in a person's life when there is the same amount of change, and the same openness to change and new views, as there is during puberty. It is no coincidence that cultural revolutions and revolts are often set in motion by students – by adolescents who no longer depend on their parents, but who have also not yet fully adjusted to the norms of adult society.

We had incredible numbers of conflicts with our children when they were adolescents. It wasn't always fun, but somehow those conflicts also seemed to "stir things up" a little, too. The children were always ready to vehemently oppose our opinions, finding ways to throw our convictions overboard. Whenever we were the slightest bit conservative, inconsistent or not entirely straightforward with them, they would immediately rub our noses in it. Where honesty or originality was concerned, we had a lot to learn from them, whether we liked it or not. I was often surprised at their eagerness to communicate with us, particularly

> when we didn't preach, but rather appealed to their
> intellect. Sometimes I thought it a shame that in a mere
> ten years they would have lost their spunk and would
> face life as tamed lions. I knew I would never be able to
> communicate as profoundly and honestly with them as
> in this period.

I will discuss the best way to appeal to a child's mental capacities
in the last three chapters, which focus on communication. For
now, and as far as this chapter is concerned, I will limit the text
to the general changes that adolescents go through. I have based
my research mainly on the works of Martine Delfos (2005a) and
Annette Heffels (2006). Although I am aware of the fact that many
adopted children do not experience "regular puberty", I think it is
important to address these general developmental tasks at length.
By knowing what is "normal", you will learn to distinguish those
aspects of your teenager's development that are different. In the
second chapter, I address adolescence and adoption specifically.

Pre-adolescence (9–12 years): changes

Physical and hormonal changes

In prepuberty, most children experience a growth spurt, which
indicates their biological coming of age. This growth spurt usually
lasts for about five years. Girls grow fastest between 11 and 13.
After that, they continue to grow at a slower pace until around 16.
In the case of boys, the growth spurt starts up a little later. They
grow fastest between 13 and 15 and, on average, keep growing
until they are 18, surpassing girls somewhere along the way
(Heffels, 2006, p.32). Growth spurts often abruptly end the
childhood years, and may have severe consequences for further
development: suddenly the child is in an adult body, although she
cannot cope with this mentally and emotionally.

This growth spurt was something extraordinary. Suddenly my little boy had a man's body. When I saw him walking down the street he almost looked like an adult, even though he was only 14. He started going his own way and became more susceptible to fashion and advertising. In discussions and fights he gained ground, but what can you do? It's difficult to mother or reprimand a boy who is a head taller than you are. He didn't like being hugged as often, either. But sometimes, very unexpectedly, he would want a hug and I would feel his tall, lanky body against mine, very odd. I also noticed a change in his contact with friends; older boys began seeing him as an equal, which of course he thought was very cool. Suddenly he was part of the in-crowd. And that brought its dangers along too. It led him into situations that did not fit his emotional age. Sometimes I think that big body of his was responsible for his seeing the wrong kind of friends. He was just too big for his age.

A pre-adolescent also finds himself in between stages sexually. She doesn't feel small any more and can communicate verbally on a seemingly adult level. On the other hand, she is not quite an adult and lacks the ability to engage in adult relationships. According to Delfos (2005a, p.49), a pre-adolescent is in a period of *paradoxical intimacy*: pushing around, pinching and fighting in the playground are her ways of exploring sexuality. Furthermore, the increase in growth hormones and sex hormones influences the mood and behaviour of the pre-adolescent.

Growth of the brain

Around the age of 11 or 12 a growth spurt occurs in the frontal lobe of the brain. Because of this, prepubescents experience a change of perspective on their world and immediate surroundings. Their thinking becomes more abstract. More and more, the child in her final years of primary school is able to form a concept of how she is perceived by others. An important element in this period (of prepubescence) is the formation of a *social identity* (see 'Psychological and social changes' below) (Delfos, 2005b, p.202).

In the field of morality, the child learns to test standards and values by her own views. Rules that were once accepted without resistance are now weighed and judged. From a moral standpoint, the prepubescent child wants to be "good". Social and ideological subjects become important. Deep emotional attachment to the contents of an ideology usually follows a few years later, during puberty. Because a child in prepubescence still "follows" her parents, and accepts things from them, this is an important time for sex education, information on drug use and giving information on the child's adoption. A prepubescent child is still open to reasoning and moral viewpoints provided by her parents.

Psychological and social changes

Between the ages of eight and 12, it is important for children to become socialised. Children of this age are open to learning how to cope with others in groups. Girls usually tend to become more confidential about their emotions, while boys tend more to "physically compare". Girls often have a few close friends, while boys tend to function in groups.

Apart from sociability, friendships have other important functions in the period of childhood development (I have based my research mainly on Delfos, 2005a, pp.65–67). Through friendships, children practise their future adult roles. Friends are equals (contrary to parents). By engaging in peer friendships, pubescent children distance themselves from adults, to whom they have to conform both at home (parents) and at school (teachers). Only in their imagination, in the privacy of their own room or in free time spent with peers, is it possible for them to self-define and open up new horizons.

- Through friendships, children practise gender-specific roles (this is especially important between the ages of nine and 12).
- Friendships provide the child with a social identity. Creating a social identity is an important developmental task for prepubescent children (see below).
- Peers provide support and solidarity. If children have a loyal group of friends they will feel supported and will feel less insecure when investigating their psychological identity during puberty (see below, 'Psychological and social changes').
- Friendships can prevent children from joining high-risk groups, or from ending up in trouble in the future. The more developed a teenager's identity, the less need there is for her to conform to peer pressure (Delfos, 2005a, p.56). Friendships improve people's sensitivity to other people's feelings.

The development of a social identity is especially important in prepubescence. If children in prepubescence can build one or more close groups of friends, they will be able to develop a positive social identity. This can be of great importance in puberty, when a child retreats into her own psychic space, looking for her own psychological identity. In a vulnerable period such as puberty, friends can provide a strong safety net and support a positive self-image.

Delfos separates identity into two parts (2005a, p.56):

- the **social identity** (how do you experience the perception others have of you)
- the **psychological identity** (how do I experience myself).

The social identity is formed between eight and 12, in the last years of primary school. Close friendships are often formed in this period, but they do not always last long. Both forming friendships and breaking them off are equally important for children's social identity. Eventually, children will learn to maintain the friendships that matter to them. The forming *and* breaking off of friendships are continuing attempts at constructing a social identity. When a child eventually learns that there are friends who appreciate her, she can develop a positive social identity. Children's psychological identity will be formed later, mainly between the ages of 12 and 18 (see below, 'Psychological and social changes').

During the final years in primary school, children also develop personal interests. They want to be accepted by the group, but they also want to distinguish themselves in ways that are attractive to the group. They do this by collecting objects or choosing a specific hobby or sport that shows their personal interest, and with which they can associate with certain other children at the same time. Also in prepubescence, children often look for idols, with whom they can identify, and also connect with other children who have the same idol.

Puberty (12–18): changes

Puberty is a repetition of the developments first seen in children at nursery school age: children break free from their parents and obtain a certain degree of independence/autonomy. This process of breaking free is often the source of tensions between children and parents. Pubescent children start to function more and more independently of their parents. This period of breaking free can be divided into four periods: 12–14 years, 14–16, 16–18 and 18 years onwards.

12–14

Teenagers in this phase are mainly in the process of maturation and growth. Huge physical and hormonal changes make them unstable. On account of teenagers' height, adults may approach them as adults, which they are not. This can be very confusing. Because peers become increasingly important, these young teenagers are influenced by group standards more than before. This is why they rebel against their parents. For the first time, they realise that they are different from their parents and will have to function on their own some day. It's best for parents to continue to monitor the developments of their teenager in this period, even though young adolescents don't appreciate this. Setting rules and creating boundaries is very important. It is also important that you remain in control and make decisions where needed.

14–16

In this second phase, teenagers experiment a lot. They think they can do anything, listen more to their friends than their parents and are ignorant of danger. To these adolescents, parents are often an obstacle on the way to independence. This period often scares parents, especially because this is the time when adolescents can suddenly start displaying risky behaviour. They barely seem to listen to their parents, and this makes it hard for parents to trust a teenager who is acting so strangely. For teenagers who have not developed a positive social identity and don't have any real friends, this is a tricky phase. Delfos writes (2005a, pp.59–60):

> From the age of 14 on, contact with peers becomes increasingly important. If the adolescent has not made friends, he runs the risk of joining high-risk groups. The codes of these high-risk groups are often clear. They have obvious rules on hairstyles, alcohol and drug use, the use of vehicles, contact with adults and speech. Accepting these rules makes joining the group easier. A lonely youth can try to join by following the rules [of the group]: and suddenly he has "friends".

Delfos definitely does not imply that this phase is problematic for all children, but there often is a certain turning-point after which children suddenly create some distance from their parents. It is vital for young adolescents to be able to experiment with their independence, but within safe limits set by their parents. Creating (limited) boundaries and providing security are a parent's most important tasks in this phase.

After this – often turbulent – phase the situation gradually returns to normal, with children developing adult behaviour that was lacking before. Delfos' main advice to parents is to 'wait this period out'. If a child has only had mild problems before puberty, chances are that these will have disappeared after this period.

16–18

After a turbulent period, adolescents often return to base in this third phase, especially because they fear losing contact with their parents altogether. Their notion of independence becomes more realistic and this might deepen the relationship with their parents.

For parents, this is often a surprising phase because it appears that the bond with their teenager, which was under threat from fights, is now suddenly becoming more profound. Adolescents have learned that they cannot be as independent as they thought they could – and this often leads to a renewed appreciation of their parents.

For families that have experienced intense confrontations in the last phase, in which their teenager may have run away from home or moved out completely, this phase can be difficult. The teenager is often afraid of her parent's anger, while the parents may have been hurt so badly and feel used to such an extent that they cannot see this approach as a phase of development. In order to strengthen the parent–child relationship, it is necessary for parents to recognise this phase and provide their child with enough space to return home "with honour".

18 years and on

Finally, a phase of strengthening takes place, and your teenager will grow into a young adult with a sense of personal identity. In this period, your child develops her own ideas and strengthens her choices in order to make well-founded decisions.

Physical and hormonal changes

In prepubescence and puberty, moods and behaviour are influenced by radical changes in the child's hormonal production: growth hormones cause explosive growth, and sex hormones cause the ripening of genitalia. Because these hormonal productions are subject to big shifts, almost every teenager goes through mood swings, the intensity of which depends on heredity and circumstances. For girls, these mood swings are not restricted to puberty, but will remain present during the menstrual cycle. Mood swings and behavioural problems in teenagers are therefore often caused by strongly fluctuating hormonal production.

> The hardest part for me was that my daughter could be so unpredictable in those days. She could be happy with a grade she got one day, and utterly dissatisfied with it the next, after she'd compared it to her friends' grades. It was impossible to predict what her mood would be like. One day she would be in tears because her boyfriend had broken up with her and the world seemed to come to an end, the next it seemed as if she did not really care.

Many more changes take place under the influence of growth hormones. Sexuality becomes a preoccupation, and children develop their sexual identity: heterosexual, homosexual, bisexual or transsexual. Children also start to feel more developed psychologically: parental dominance – based in part on their physical superiority – becomes less obvious as children grow physically.

Brain growth

During puberty, major cognitive changes take place. In a short period of time, the brain develops many new synapses by which adolescents gain greater understanding. Suddenly they are able to see connections between things that appeared to them as separate facts before. They are now capable of thinking in abstract and systematic ways, are able to concentrate for longer periods of time and can empathise with others and reflect upon themselves. This sudden growth causes a feeling of euphoria in the adolescent, who is proud of her newly gained insights and is sure she now understands everything. She will start to look at her social environment in a more critical and detached way, and will eagerly test her newly gained insights on her parents and society. Family/house rules are no longer unquestioned, and moral opinions and social ideals become important themes.

> When my brothers and I were in our teens, there would be daily debates and arguments, especially about politics, because that was a hot issue back then – for us as well as our parents. My parents were right-wingers, so naturally we were left-wing. My friends were too – with them I felt a strong connection. Discussions with my dad were most satisfying. I was always out to win a debate. We fought frequently, because it was impossible to agree, of course. I didn't mind as much as my father, though. I was extremely ambitious in those days. A hunger for knowledge drove me to new insights and viewpoints, and preferably ones contrary to my parents. I wanted badly for them to see who I was, to accept my ideas, and to be proud of my understanding.

Although a teenager's brain is developing intensively, it needs some time to be re-organised and re-structured; this is why teenagers cannot always manage the consequences of their actions and ideas. It is important for you as the parent to help your teenager to make the necessary connections, to keep your child out of harm's way, and to make sure he or she gets enough sleep, eats a healthy diet and – if at all possible – finishes school.

Psychological and social changes

Ideally, a child has created a social identity by the time she leaves primary school (What do others think of me?). During puberty, the steep descent into the self begins, and makes children look for their psychological identity (What do I think of myself?). For a healthy descent into the self, it is important for a child to have enough confidence. Preferably this self-esteem was built up in earlier stages. With a certain amount of autonomy, secure attachments and a positive social identity will allow a child to establish closer friendships through which she can experience support and solidarity from peers. In early adolescence, empathy and helpfulness are central aspects of friendships; as children develop, the emphasis shifts toward emotional aspects such as loyalty, confidentiality and being able to be oneself (Delfos, 2005a, p.67).

In order to function well in society, the ability to engage in satisfactory relationships with others is not the only requirement; it is equally important for adolescents to become independent from their parents. Eventually, teenagers must be able to make their own decisions and take responsibility for their lives. To get to that stage, it is important that they acquire insight into their own personality, so they can develop a psychological identity that suits them. It is for good reason, then, that adolescents in this period of their lives question their surroundings – rules, opinions and moral values. In their search for their own adult identity, teenagers will alternately be very close to their parents or keep them at a distance. Adolescents ask themselves questions such as, 'Who am I? What can I do? What direction will I take?' And the only way for them to find answers to these questions is for them to reflect deeply upon themselves, in search of their own deepest motives and the foundations of their existence. It is rare for people to reflect upon themselves as thoroughly and lastingly as they do in puberty. Subjects that did not seem important before are able to induce crises during this time.

Psychological identity includes among other things (Delfos, 2005a, p.58):

- sexual identity (am I homo-, hetero-, bi- or transsexual?)
- cultural identity (to what culture do I belong and how am I to behave in it?)
- intellectual identity (how do I experience my own intellect? In other words, what am I capable of?)
- spiritual identity (to what religious or spiritual movement do I belong?).

Adolescents often "try on" several identities in order to determine who they really are. Questions about these identities often continue to play a role for the rest of a person's life.

Parents: changes

A lot changes for parents during their child's puberty. The most obvious change is probably your teenager's rapid metamorphosis into an autonomous being who questions your advice and rules. Suddenly, you as a parent are no longer the most important person in the world, but instead will receive blunt criticism and will no longer be seen as an authority.

> Suddenly everything in my daughter's life was about her friends, not about us. She was constantly calling and instant-messaging/texting her friends. Only when she needed money or if there was trouble would she ask for our help. When I told her she couldn't do some things or should do others, it would almost always result in opposition. I noticed that I needed to approach her differently, address her as an equal, which I found very difficult, especially in the beginning. I was so used to her being my "child", and her being dependent on me. Just like my daughter, I had to free myself from the symbiotic, co-dependent relationship that had been so obvious before. Perhaps it was harder for me than for my daughter.

Not until you accept that your role as a parent is permanently changing, will your teenager be able to develop freely towards adulthood. It can be helpful to investigate to what extent possible feelings of insecurity are projections of one's own pain. I will look at this in Chapter 6. It can also help to understand what phases of development your teenager must go through, so you can place her behaviour in a wider context. Young adults need to reach the following goals (Akkerman and colleagues, 2004, in Delfos, 2005a, p.32):

- they are able to make decisions for themselves and carry responsibility;
- they can spend their spare time in useful and appropriate ways;
- they are able to choose a job or further education that is suitable for them;
- they can look after their health and appearance;
- they can keep up friendships and take others into account;
- they are able to acknowledge there are rules that they must follow;
- they are able to engage in relationships of intimacy and sexuality;
- they can live on their own, separate from their parents.

By understanding the goals your teenager must achieve, you can probably understand and accept her behaviour better. Possibly, you may help her better in achieving those goals.

Adoptive families are confronted with certain additional changes in puberty. These changes affect you and your teenager alike. I will address these changes in the chapters ahead.

Factors that influence an adolescent's development

Predisposition, circumstances/history and the parenting situation

The factors that influence the behaviour of adolescents are fairly complex. There is never a single obvious cause for the fact that an adolescent does not develop in the best possible way. Usually, it is the result of a combination of factors associated with:

- predisposition;
- the circumstances (history) in which the child is brought up;
- the parenting situation.

Heffels calls this 'the three-factor model'. (I based the theory mentioned mainly on Heffels, 2006, pp.58–62. I have personally filled in the definition of childhood circumstances, based upon Delfos' developmental theories and my own knowledge of the subject – see also Wolfs, 2008.)

Predisposition

The child's genetic predisposition plays an important role in her development. *Intelligence*, *aptitude* and *abilities* determine the developmental possibilities to a large extent.

Temperament is also an important aspect. Therefore, every child deals differently with adversity: some become combative and strong, others become passive and vulnerable. A vulnerable child who loses someone close or who goes through their parents' divorce will react differently than a strong, resilient child going through the same experiences. A child's degree of resilience is heavily determined by temperament: is a child open and optimistic, or is she more introverted and pessimistic by nature?

Emotional strength, or resilience, is determined by the following characteristics, according to Heffels:

- being optimistic versus being melancholy/pessimistic;
- being emotionally stable versus being emotionally unstable/easily upset;
- being outgoing versus being introverted;

- being careful/precise versus being sloppy/easily distracted;
- having initiative, being active versus being passive.

It is not a question of the child having or lacking these characteristics but rather of the *extent* to which a child has them. Most people lean towards a certain type of personality, but they never fit the profile one hundred per cent. A child's development is also influenced by other aspects of predisposition, such as intelligence, aptitude and abilities, as noted above.

Circumstances/history

A second factor that influences children's development is their circumstances. It is, for example, very important what *place* the child holds *within the family*: is she an only child, the eldest, middle or youngest child? The temperaments of the child's siblings can also have a strong influence on her development, as can *important life events* that take place in the family. The death of a parent or sibling will have a major effect on a child's development. The same is true for frequent moves or a divorce, or if the child is in a school where she doesn't feel she belongs. Adopted children and foster children have often known two different situations: one with their birth parents or in an institution, and another with their adoptive or foster parents. Of course, their history has an impact on their development. I will address this in following chapters.

Parenting situation

The parenting situation plays an important role in the child's development. Contrary to predisposition and circumstances, this factor can be affected by you as a parent. It is possible, for instance, for you to create the conditions that will nurture your teenager's healthy development. A substantial part of these conditions will be shaped *before* puberty: if your child has already passed through certain important *developmental stages*, this contributes considerably to a healthy development from adolescence into adulthood. In the next section, I discuss some of these vital stages more extensively.

Another important contribution that you can make as a parent to your child's upbringing is that you are willing to reflect on your own thoughts and feelings and that you question your own behaviour if necessary. If you understand who you are yourself and why you have become the way you are, you will be able to look at your child more open-mindedly and to assist her more freely and positively in the process of going through her developmental tasks (see also Chapter 6).

You can also help your teenager to develop by teaching yourself specific communicative and didactic skills, which will allow you to be more in touch with your child's inner world. I will discuss the skills that can help you to achieve this in the last three chapters.

If you want to understand why your child is developing well or why she experiences problems, you are advised to look at the three above-mentioned factors (predisposition, circumstances/history, parenting situation). According to Heffels, there is hardly ever just one single obvious cause for developmental problems. She writes (Heffels, 2006, p.62):

> To understand why a child develops into an independent, well-functioning (more or less), happy adult, or to understand why certain problems arise, you need a model with a minimum of three factors. Predisposition, parenting situation and circumstances have to be taken into account. Additionally, there is a correlation between these three factors. They influence one another. Simple explanations such as 'it's because he was sick a lot when he was small', or 'he has inherited his mother's sensitivity', or 'this is a result of his parent's divorce' will not suffice.

The chances of your child developing in a healthy way are generally strongest under positive circumstances and in a favourable parenting situation.

In connection with this, it is obvious that the development of adopted children will often be more complicated simply because of their history. A recent meta-analysis by van IJzendoorn and Juffer (2006) showed that around 53 per cent of all adopted children appear not to have bonded securely. It is quite possible, therefore, that you only partially recognise "normal development" in your adopted or foster child(ren). Because it is important to be aware of what is considered "normal", I have based this chapter on the general development of adolescents. Specific problems in adoptive situations are addressed extensively in later chapters.

Basic aspects of development before puberty

As I mentioned in the last section, the completion or incompletion of specific developmental tasks can influence the development of your child. Being aware of these age-bound tasks will allow you to be attentive to them, which can have a positive influence on the development of your teenager into an adult.

The most important developmental tasks of an adolescent are all connected to the maturing process. In the end, children must be able to act independently, make autonomous decisions and take responsibility. They should be able to answer the following questions: 'Who am I? What am I capable of? What direction do I want to take?' Besides that, they must be able to form satisfactory relationships with others. They should be able to take care of themselves, and also they need to take others into account and accept differences between people.

In order to make use of this knowledge and these skills as adults, children have to complete certain developmental tasks in different categories of age. These tasks are age-bound. Most of them have been basically developed *before* puberty. I now discuss several (but certainly not all) basic, though important, aspects of healthy development. (This paragraph is based on Delfos, *Ik heb ook wat te vertellen*, 2005a, p.87 e.v..)

Secure bonds, positive self-image, autonomy: 0–6 years

Ideally, a child has developed secure bonds and a positive self-image before her fifth or sixth year. She must also have acquired a certain level of autonomy (independence) and been taught positive moral values.

Knowledge of biological origins: 6–8 years

Between the ages of six and eight, it is important for children to learn about their biological origins. Delfos writes (2005a, p.90):

> In this phase a child starts to see through concepts and will take an interest in the composition of the family and in his or her heritage. A familiar question in this period is: But where was I when you were in grandma's tummy?

Around this time, adopted children start to wonder where they come from, who their birth parents are and why they were adopted. Their heritage starts to play a more important role, just like the story of their conception and birth.

Building a positive social identity: 8–12 years

During this period, a child ideally forms a positive social identity ('others like me, people love me and I have pretty cool friends'). That is why it is important for children of this age to learn how to interact with peers in groups.

At this age, they are also the most open to receiving information on sexuality and drugs. According to Delfos, it is important to give this information at the end of primary school, not at the beginning of puberty, because children of 11 or 12 are open to social values and to social problems. They want to be "good" in the eyes of society. Providing sex education and information about drugs at this time may have a preventive effect, as sexuality and drug use become important matters for children during puberty.

Most of the above-mentioned developmental tasks are repeated and expanded in puberty. If one of these tasks is insufficiently developed before puberty, chances are it will come up as a problem during puberty.

Developing autonomy, for instance, is one of the main tasks in puberty, for which foundations are laid in infancy. If a child has achieved a sufficient level of autonomy as a toddler (during the first recalcitrant phase at the age of 2–3 years), this can partially determine the course of the second recalcitrant phase (16–17 years).

For another core task during puberty, establishing relations with peers, the foundations have also been laid in earlier phases. Children cannot establish healthy relations unless or until they have developed secure bonds and constructed a positive social identity. A positive social identity can be an important protective factor in puberty, and can be of great importance in forming a psychological identity; in fact, a positive social identity works as a safety net during puberty (Delfos, 2005a, p.84). The knowledge of biological origins also deepens during puberty. And finally, the moral values that have been passed on to a child before her 12th year help her to make choices between good and bad, and with problems concerning addictive behaviour.

Creating conditions for healthy development before and during puberty

As I noted before, you can create conditions for your teenager's healthy development not only during puberty, but also before. I will summarise a number of these conditions below.

If possible, give your child opportunities to form secure bonds before her fifth or sixth year. A child who has developed secure attachments and reached a certain level of autonomy as an infant and toddler, will show her true self more readily (and show both positive and negative emotions), will be better able to form close relationships and will reach a more natural independence and autonomy in puberty.

When your child is six to eight years old, take more time to talk about her origins. Tell her where she came from and who her parents were/are; also re-tell the story of her conception and birth. At this time, children are responsive to learning about their heritage. If they can deal with questions about their identity such as, 'Who am I? Who do I resemble? How do I fit into the genetic line of my family? In what aspects am I unique?', they can more naturally add an extra dimension to their identity during puberty.

Between the ages of eight and 12, children form their social identity. Provide your child with opportunities to build strong friendships in this period. Close friendships with peers teach children that others see them in a favourable light. This positive self-image provides a good social safety net in the vulnerable years of puberty, when teenagers contemplate their psychological identity.

Children feel most secure when they have a clear structure and basic rules to live by during their upbringing. Apart from making them feel secure, rules also help children to grow up in a healthy way and to learn that not every demand can be immediately satisfied. This teaches them to build up a strong frustration tolerance, which will be to their advantage in adulthood. Children with a high frustration tolerance level, as a rule, become less egocentric and will be less focused on gratification as adults. Moreover, these children usually develop more perseverance and are better able to "cope with life", in which dealing with adversity is an important factor.

Children develop best when they have built up enough basic trust and have an appropriate self-image, one that is realistic. They build up basic trust when their parents create a sensitive parenting situation. If parents respond sensitively to behaviour and emotions, children learn that they can show their needs, emotions and thoughts, and that they do not have to display adjusted/desirable behaviour or strong resistance. It is important for you to keep paying attention to this during puberty. Communication based on respect, sensitivity and reciprocity will benefit your adolescent's development. Besides, you will have better access to your teenager's world by communicating well. I will cover this extensively in the last three chapters.

Although adolescents need fewer rules than young children, a (limited) set of rules is of great importance to them. For them to develop well, it is very important that they eat a healthy diet, get enough sleep and finish school. They also need rules to ensure their safety (for example, that they do not mix with unknown groups or spend the night at an unfamiliar place). In a television series on Dutch teenagers (taken from the article 'Geweldloos verzet als remedie tegen rebelse pubers', *De Standaard*, 16-02-2005), 16-year-old Emmy puts it like this:

> When I was 13 I used to go to town with friends. It did not matter [to my parents] what time I came home. So I would say, 'Shall I be home by two, Mum? Two is alright, don't you think?' I thought there ought to be a rule, so I would set one myself.

Creating (some) boundaries and rules is particularly important because your teenager may well act like an adult, but isn't one yet.

Her brain is not quite fully grown, so she might not be capable of taking responsibility for the causes and consequences of certain actions. Clear rules can protect your teenager against reckless and unsafe behaviour.

It is important that you, as a parent, know and understand yourself and that you are aware of the influence of your temperament on that of your child. If you are aware of this, there is a greater chance that you can influence your child positively.

Heffels (2006, p.49) describes this as follows:

> A child's temperament and predisposition have an effect on the parents and the parenting situation, and vice versa – the temperament and predisposition of the parents influence the child. Consequently, there is an interaction between these two factors. A spunky father may therefore have some difficulty with a passive son. He could respond by teaching his son to show more spunk or by becoming impatient with him. This would force the son too much. Both parties influence each other (consciously and unconsciously).

Additionally, it is important that you are aware of your own life history and the patterns of behaviour that follow from it. When you are well acquainted with your own prejudices and fears, and are willing to accept them as yours, you are less likely to pass them on to your child. This will put less of a burden on your child's shoulders and your child will not be "contaminated" with your history.

Conclusion

In this chapter I have given a general sketch of the developmental changes that adolescents go through, and of the influences that affect those changes. Adoptive families will encounter additional changes, and, in the following chapters, I elaborate on these.

2

Puberty and adoption

There is, in short, no "right" or "wrong" way to experience being adopted... But if you are adopted, you will think about that fact of your life now and again – maybe when a question arises about your genetic background, maybe when you encounter a particularly rough spot in your life, maybe every single day.
David M Brodzinsky (1992)

Introduction

There is hardly a teenager who passes through puberty without confrontations. Changes in body and brain take place so fast and intensely, it is almost impossible for a child to experience these in tranquillity. Puberty is especially complex for adopted teenagers, mainly because they have to base a large part of the development of their identity on an adoption history, and the genetic connection to parents that they do not know (or do not know well). Questions that are important to them are: 'Who were my parents, and who am I? Were my parents bad people, and does that mean I have bad genes?' Questions such as 'Did my birth mother love me? Why did she part with me? Was I wanted? Did my parents love each other? Should I have been here?' will play an important role in their lives and influence their self-image. Because their brains are beginning to understand the adoption story on deeper levels, adopted teenagers start asking themselves questions about the past. As a consequence, many adopted children start grieving over their adoption (again) and are confronted with feelings of shame, fear, anger and guilt.

In addition, adopted teenagers are especially sensitive to abandonment in puberty – when they are expected to become independent. They can also start to feel more insecure at school and with friends because they are different from their non-adopted peers.

Because adopted children need the most satisfactory answers possible to their questions and thoughts, they often go through an intense and vulnerable puberty. They are, even more so than "regular" teenagers, in need of sensitive parents with sufficient basic trust and self-knowledge, who can empathise with their teenager's feelings and not be blown over too soon. It can, however, for several reasons be difficult for you as an adoptive parent to provide that stability. Your teenager's intense puberty can be very confrontational for you too. Particularly when your child starts displaying behaviour that conflicts with your personal values, truths and expectations, you may start hearing the echoes of friends and acquaintances warning you ten or 15 years earlier that raising adopted children "who are not your own" was likely to cause trouble. As a consequence of your teenager's irresponsible or aggressive behaviour, you may start to fear the your child has "bad genes" and you may start fantasising about what it would have been like to have had birth children. Many of the fears and uncertainties that played a role before the adoption will surface in this phase: 'Am I a good mother/father? Would my child rather be with his birth parents? If only we were a "normal" family. What would it have been like to have a birth child? We have to make our child happy. Soon he will leave home and we will be alone again.'

Especially in this hectic period full of change, it is likely that you and your teenager will touch on each other's vulnerabilities and influence each other's emotions more heavily than either of you might want to. Perhaps you have both been damaged by feelings of loss in the past; as a result, you can both be more susceptible to rejection, loss and abandonment. You both might also feel you have to be a super-parent or super-child, or you might feel vulnerable about not having a genetic bond.

To provide your teenager with the space he needs to develop well, it is important that you gain an insight into your teenager's thoughts and emotions as well as into your own. In this chapter, I therefore outline the additional topics that often occupy the minds of both the adopted teenager and the adoptive parent (my research is partially based on Riley, 2005). Then, in the section 'Adoption-related grief' I elaborate on the difficult grieving process that adopted children may go through as a consequence of these additional topics.

A different concern, but recognisable especially in intercountry adoptions, is "premature puberty". Because this subject is separate from the socio-emotional issues covered in the 'Additional topics for adopted teenagers' and 'Additional topics for parents', I discuss it first.

Premature puberty

Although many adopted children reach puberty at roughly the same age as non-adopted children, there is a greater possibility that they will reach puberty earlier. This acceleration of physical development is probably due to the transition from a limited diet in their country of birth to more versatile nutrition in their adoptive country. Because development in boys and girls is different, I will treat them separately when necessary (for this theme I have based my research mainly on documentation provided by Basic Trust, Janet Gooden, 2003a and 2003b).

Girls

Generally speaking, girls reach puberty one year before boys do. On average, they are ten years old when they reach puberty and they have their first period when they are 13.3 years old. Internationally adopted girls can reach puberty between eight and ten years old, or even earlier. On average, they start menstruating when they are 12. If the hormonal system in the brain matures too early, children reach puberty prematurely. Puberty is considered premature if a girl starts to develop breasts before her eighth birthday, or when she starts menstruating before her ninth birthday. Signs of the onset of puberty *can* be:

- your daughter is developing breasts or is experiencing sensitivity around the nipples;
- her body odour is more mature;
- the shape of her body is changing: fatty tissue is gathering around her hips, buttocks, upper arms and thighs; her pelvis is widening and her face is growing fuller;
- she is developing pubic hair and hair in her armpits;
- she is going through a growth spurt (this can result in a growth of 11–12 centimetres per year); the growth spurt usually starts two years before her first menstruation; after menstruation has started girls usually only grow about five or six more centimetres.

Boys

Boys usually reach puberty when about 11 years old. Internationally adopted boys sometimes start puberty before their eleventh year. What goes for girls, goes for boys too: if the hormonal system in the brain matures too quickly, they reach puberty prematurely. Puberty is considered premature when the penis and testicles grow before the boy's ninth birthday. Signs of the onset of puberty *can* be:

- your son's penis and testicles are growing;
- his bone structure is becoming more pronounced;

- he is developing an adult body odour;
- he is developing pubic hair, hair on his chest or in his armpits.

Later on in puberty, the following features appear:

- your son's voice is breaking;
- your son is experiencing a growth spurt (this happens later in boys than in girls);
- his first ejaculation takes place.

Consequences of premature puberty

A premature puberty can have both physical and socio-emotional consequences. Socio-emotionally, children may become unbalanced. They might:

- become rebellious;
- try to gain more autonomy;
- develop adolescent interests;
- fall deeply in love with a classmate;
- become insecure and afraid because they cannot relate completely to their peers;
- be ashamed because they are developing breasts or a large penis, or have pubic hair;
- be approached sexually by older children because they look older than they are.

Physically, a premature puberty means children *stop growing early* and might not reach their potential height. Because internationally adopted children are very often smaller than their peers, it can be useful to consult a doctor or paediatric endocrinologist. There are treatments for postponing puberty that will make it possible for your child's body to continue to grow.

If you notice any of the abovementioned characteristics of premature puberty in your child, you would be wise to make an appointment with your GP and ask for a referral to a paediatrician or a paediatric endocrinologist. If the latter has little experience with adopted children, she or he should be able to contact paediatric endocrinologists in academic hospitals, who are often more than happy to share their knowledge.

If your child has a problem with his final height or prematurely changing body, you can consult an adoption support worker.

Additional issues for adopted teenagers

Probably it isn't always easy for you as a parent to distinguish between "normal" problems of puberty or your child's personality, and problems related to his adoption history. To get a better grip on this, I will discuss several issues that adopted teenagers are often confronted with in different phases. Possibly you will recognise these in your teenager and be able to guide him safely on the road to adulthood.

By periodically working through these issues, adopted teenagers are able to understand their adoption history on a deeper level and can connect with the past as well as the present, step by step.

Identity

Forming an identity is not an easy task for any adolescent. Every teenager has to discover what differences and similarities there are between himself and his parents. For adolescents, who are mentally and physically confronted with many changes, this is often an emotional process. They are all in search of their personal preferences and their own strengths and weaknesses. Their identity is gradually formed by genetics (such as aptitude, intellectual abilities, ethnic background, physical characteristics) and by environmental factors. Environmental factors are defined by the family in which they are raised (for example, they are formed by the family values, culture, status, social surroundings and the way

parents and friends perceive them) and by what they have
experienced (loss, trauma, etc).

Adopted children should not only be able to compare themselves
with their adoptive parents but also (and sometimes especially)
with their birth parents, because these are an integral part of
their identity. Because they may know next to nothing about their
genetic background, it is often quite difficult for these teenagers
to form an identity. They can, for example, be afraid of having
inherited "bad genes" (for example, sexual or aggressive behaviour)
from their birth parents, resulting in the development of a negative
self-image. They also do not know what their birth parents think,
or thought, of them. Because these parents have put them up for
adoption at a young age, many adopted children believe their birth
parents think negatively of them. Moreover, internationally adopted
children often feel caught between cultures, which leads to
difficulty in integrating both cultures into one identity. An adopted
teenager has to integrate two pairs of parents and possibly two
cultures; he needs to find out how he is different and how he is
similar. This unknown background can lead to an "empty" feeling
in adopted teenagers.

Reason for adoption

As I wrote above, adopted children need to be able to compare
themselves with both pairs of parents in order to develop their
own identity. Besides that, it is important for their self-image to
know what both pairs of parents think of them. One of the most
important questions that they need an answer to at this time is *why*
they were put up for adoption: 'Why did my birth parents not want
me? Was it my fault that I was put up for adoption? Wasn't I good
enough? What does this say about me? Did my birth parents love
each other? Should I have been here? Are my birth parents still
alive? Are they sorry that I'm gone? Do they miss me?' Adopted
teenagers often react with anger towards their "abandonment".
They realise perfectly well that "normal" parents love their children

and that they take care of them and protect them. Why didn't their birth mother do that? Nothing hurts as much as a voluntary abandonment or separation. And however often they mull over it, it usually leads to nothing, because in most cases there just isn't a straightforward answer. Others decided for them when they were still small, the adoption is irreversible and the reasons for it are unclear. Because there is no resolution to this situation, it is often very difficult for adopted teenagers to grieve over this fact of life in a healthy way. Sometimes they are filled with blind rage about what was done to them. The underlying pain in many cases is the result of that first rejection, for which the reason is unknown or painful. It is important that people who are adopted are given the chance to grieve over this (see 'Adoption-related grief').

Missing information

Adoptees in puberty increasingly need more detailed facts about the looks, personalities and lives of the people who put them on this earth. Because they want to proceed in their development, they need (once again) to learn detailed facts about their past so they can be processed. They are now cognitively capable of processing painful information at a deeper level and to look at it from different angles. As a result of this, emotions like sadness, shame, fear, anger and aggression can arise. Traumatic events can also (re-)surface. Because these facts are being processed from a different perspective than before, it can take a lot of energy to deal with them (again). Although (possibly new) painful facts can give rise to many emotions, adopted teenagers benefit in their development from knowing the facts. When they finally learn the truth, many adopted children say that 'they had always sensed it'. The facts may hurt but the truth is often seen as liberating. At last they understand their own (unconscious) behaviour or feelings and can make a realistic connection with the past. Uncertain or indeterminate feelings or unrealistic thoughts can be let go of, and as a result of this they will be able to use their energy in more productive ways. Through knowing the facts they will be able to construct more realistic fantasies and shape their identity in a better way.

Loyalty

To be able to develop well, adopted teenagers have to disconnect from their adoptive parents on the one hand and connect with their birth parents on the other. This is a complicated task, especially because adopted children often feel they aren't allowed to disconnect from (rebel against) their adoptive parents because they provided them with a better life. Besides that, they often feel guilty for fantasising about or longing for their birth parents because they feel that, in doing so, they are rejecting their adoptive parents. In many cases, adopted teenagers experience all these contradictory thoughts about both pairs of parents in secret, because they do not want to hurt their adoptive parents. By not sharing their thoughts with their parents, they often get caught up in an even stronger conflict of loyalties. It may be that adopted teenagers are not consciously aware of being engaged in this inner conflict; for example, they may only experience feelings of dissatisfaction or may strongly rebel against their adoptive parents, but they do not know the underlying reasons. Deep inside there can still be a longing for their birth parents.

Adopted teenagers are much better off when they know from the start that it is OK for them to love both pairs of parents, and that there are no restrictions attached to their longings. They are also better off knowing that they do not owe their adoptive parents any gratitude, and that they are allowed, like any other teenager, to rebel against them. In the same way, you can make it clear to your child that you are just as grateful that he came into your life. To feel confident enough to rebel, adopted children in any case need enough basic trust.

Differences

Adopted teenagers need to learn to cope with the fact that they are different from other children and families in several ways. Especially in puberty, similarities between friends play an important role. Adopted children, however, are confronted with the many ways in which they are different from their peer group: they often look different, come from a different ethnic and cultural background and have a different kind of relationship with their parents because they are not their birth parents. Moreover, cognitive differences within the adoptive family may become apparent at this time. Identifying with the family in which they grow up can thus become more difficult. At school they may be confronted with values that are different from the ones at home, and this, too, can add to the confusion. Feelings of insecurity and the need to belong may cause them to join high-risk groups or to engage in sexual activity.

Awareness of these differences can have a strong influence on the adopted teenager's self-image and self-esteem. During this period of time, they need their parents to recognise and verbalise these differences and give them the opportunity to identify with a more suitable environment. Perhaps your adopted teenager fits better in a soccer team than in a field-hockey team. Maybe he'd rather play pop music instead of classical music. At the same time, it is vital to let your adopted teenager know that he is an undisputable part of the family.

Fear of desertion

It is often not apparent to adopted children that their relationships with parents or friends will last. Especially in puberty, when lasting friendships become increasingly important and the end of childhood is in sight, the fear of being abandoned by friends and parents can become stronger. Adopted children have, after all, been left before. Adopted teenagers sometimes unconsciously seek extreme boundaries to see their belief confirmed that they do not count for anything and that their family and friends will leave them sooner or later. It is particularly important for these teenagers that they become aware of their fear and that they understand its origins. In this way, they will realise that their behaviour is instinctive, while at the same time they will understand that this instinctive fear is no longer valid or necessary. They can also learn to understand that their fear is quite normal. If your teenager grasps why, for example, it is hard for him to cultivate lasting friendships, he is more likely to learn strategies with which he can hang on to his friends. It is only when he understands where his conflicting feelings and behaviour stem from that he can learn to distinguish between the past and the future (see Chapters 5 and 9).

Responsibility

Adopted children often feel responsibility in many aspects of life. For different reasons, they may feel obliged to make something of their lives. They may feel responsible towards their birth parents: they often feel the need to prove that they are surely worth something, and that they are "good" children. Also, they may feel responsible towards their adoptive parents: by being successful or happy they can show their adoptive parents that they did the right thing in adopting them. Moreover, an adoptee frequently feels a responsibility towards himself: he is privileged to grow up in a rich and prosperous part of the world and has chances that he would never have had otherwise. This material wealth, which he has received through abandonment, may make him feel guilty and thus put a heavy weight on his shoulders; his birth parents probably live in poverty. It is possible that for this reason he will feel the responsibility to visit them in the future and support them financially.

It is important for adopted teenagers to learn that they can develop freely, and that they do not need to take responsibility for everything that has happened in their lives. It is also healthy for them to learn that they only have to live up to their own expectations, not to those of their birth or adoptive parents. Of course, it is acceptable for your child to have a sense of responsibility, but that feeling should be the product of an autonomous need, and not the result of feelings of shame, guilt or fear.

Additional issues for parents

As an adoptive parent, you are likely to know very well that puberty is more complicated for your child. The emotional impact of the adoption is, after all, very significant at this stage. Therefore, it is important to know what issues your teenager is dealing with. It is, however, just as important to understand your own emotions during this hectic period. After all, your own responsive patterns can have a significant influence on the development of your child. The following may be specific topics for adoptive parents with children going through puberty.

Identity

It is likely that from the very beginning you have been confronted in several ways with the notion that 'you are not real parents'. This feeling may have been confirmed or strengthened by:

- the fact that your child is 'someone else's child';
- the fact that your child, when in a rage, yells that he will one day return to his native country or that he needn't listen to you because you aren't his real parents anyway;
- the fact that outsiders may say things such as, 'Eventually he will go looking for his real parents of course' or 'Do you know his real mother and father?';
- the fact of your possible infertility, which may lead you to think the role of a parent was never really intended for you and you might subconsciously conclude from this that you can never be a real/good parent;

- the fact that your child has a different genetic background than you, and, in this sense, really is different.

For all these reasons, it might be hard for you to cling to your autonomous identity as a parent. However it is put, there will never be genuine blood ties and right from the start you are possibly reminded of this fact by your child as well as by outsiders. In puberty, it can be especially difficult to continue to believe in the unconditional bond between you and your child. You might develop a heightened sensitivity for rejection and you may fear that in the long term you will not be accepted by your child as his "real" parents.

Reason to adopt

When adopted teenagers suddenly start asking a lot of questions about their adoption, and frequently feel angry or sad about it, parents often (re-)experience feelings of guilt: 'Was it really necessary for us to adopt a child? Was our selfish wish to become parents ever in the child's interest? Perhaps he would have been happier in his native country.' Suddenly, echoes may resound of friends and family warning you ten or 15 years earlier that raising adopted children would cause trouble. Your teenager's problematic behaviour seems to confirm these old prejudices. There is a chance that you will start to doubt your parenting skills, and might feel ambivalent towards your child, at a time when it is of the greatest importance to him that your support is unconditional. At the root of your child's extreme behaviour probably lies a lot of pain that he does not (yet) display as such.

Missing information: clarity

One of the most difficult tasks that you will come up against as an adoptive parent is to explain the story of the adoption to your child. You will not want to upset your child unnecessarily, and if the facts are very painful, this will perhaps make you keep some facts from him for the time being. Up until puberty this may have been a realistic option, because basic information was all your child needed. But in puberty this changes; most adopted children need more depth, making a revision of the story necessary. If your fears cause you to withhold painful information, this will now clearly stand in the way of your child's development. Your child will start filling in the missing information for himself, resulting in the formation of an inaccurate or inappropriate identity. Moreover, from your silence he will deduce that it is wrong to think or talk about his history, with all sorts of consequences.

Although it may seem that telling your child about painful facts is inhumane, it is in fact the most humane thing you can do for him. The story of adoption is always central in the lives of adoptive families; if you are able to give meaning to this story together with your child, however painful, this is the most honest and meaningful thing you can do for him. Only when he knows the facts, will he be able to connect with the past and the present.

Loyalty

In order to develop an identity, adopted teenagers want to know more about their birth parents. They often start thinking about those "other parents" when the possibility of a meeting comes closer: 'What would it be like to meet them?' During this process, adopted teenagers try to strike a balance between the love they feel for their adoptive parents and the growing longing to find out more about their birth parents. Perhaps you feel insecure about your child's longing; he is changing quickly and will be independent in a couple of years. A possible meeting with the birth parents becomes more realistic, and suddenly you may sense a competitiveness with the other, "more real" parents, especially when there are conflicts. For this reason, it might be tempting to keep the birth parents at a distance. Your teenager, however, will probably instinctively sense this, and feel that your position confirms that he is, indeed, prohibited from being curious about his birth parents. There is the risk of self-fulfilling prophecy in your fear that the secret feelings for his birth parents will become so intense that he will begin to believe that he would indeed be better off with them instead of with you. In such cases, it is important for you, as a parent, to express your fear of these other parents, and to make it clear that it will be difficult for you to let your child go in the future. There are no relationships without difficulties and fears, but that does not mean there won't be a lifelong connection. By expressing your own fears, it will be easier for your teenager to show his own loyalty conflict or fear of desertion, and you may find out that many shared issues even strengthen the bond between you.

Differences

In puberty, differences begin to play a greater role for your teenager as well as for you. Your child will start to search for his identity and for a group of friends to match it. Often the genetic differences between you now surface. The arguments may worsen because your teenager, for example, is more hot tempered than you are, or because he enjoys loud music, parties and noisy friends. Suddenly, he has different types of friends and his language becomes coarse, or he will start solving problems by using violence or verbal aggression. Perhaps you will feel a slight disappointment because your child is so different from your friends' children. 'What would it be like if we had children of our own? They would probably be more like us.' The desire to have a "normal" family, with "normal" (i.e., genetically related) children, can be very strong at such times. Your teenager, who feels different anyway, probably intuitively senses your desire and disappointment and may, as a result, feel confirmed in the belief that he does not belong in this family. Feelings of not being accepted may thus increase.

Fear of desertion

Growing towards independence is a natural process for children, but it isn't for their parents. For them, it seems such a short time ago that their child was small and needed his parents for warmth and security. Now this same child is rapidly growing towards adulthood, and is making preparations for his own life. The end of the most important period in the life of parents is in sight. Although children, too, are sometimes uncertain about this process, it is mostly the parents who will soon have to search actively for a new (parental) role. They will also need to renew their bond with their partner, and renegotiate the goals that they set for themselves and in relation to society. The empty-nest syndrome can bother parents for a long stretch of time. In fact, puberty puts parents and children on edge. Delfos opens her book on communicating with adolescents with the following line, for obvious reasons: 'This house is not a hotel, you only come around for meals and a bed to sleep in.' According to Delfos, this illustrates the parent's damaged ego. The adolescent wants distance, and starts acting accordingly.

Adoptive parents often, just like adopted children, have an unusual sensibility towards this process of distancing and letting go. Possibly you will think silently that your child will soon go looking for his "real parents" and that you will be alone once more. The fear of losing a child again, as you may have experienced earlier for a much-wanted birth child, can start over again. Your fear may act as a catalyst: your child, who is also afraid of being alone again soon, will instinctively sense your fear and feel confirmed in his anticipation that you will both be alone again soon. He might, for example, (unconsciously) think: 'If my adoptive parents feels the same way, then it must be true.'

Responsibility

Adoptive parents step into the process of parenting with much more awareness than birth parents usually do. Having children for them has not been straightforward; they have gone through a lot of effort to become parents. The training they have had has often made them aware of the responsibilities that they take on as adoptive parents. When, at last, they go to collect their child, they are often very much aware of the problems that adoption can bring with it. The long road to parenthood has often made adoptive parents highly motivated to provide their child with all the opportunities he needs. Besides this, they often feel extra responsibility because they are raising another parent's child. A feeling of gratitude for being able to raise this child can create a strong sense of responsibility in adoptive parents. They often expect themselves to be "super-parents". Although this sense of responsibility is understandable, and at times can be very beneficial to the development of the adopted child, it can also be dangerous. After all, children want to live up to their parents' expectations. If those expectations are high out of a sense of responsibility, it is very difficult for a child to allow himself the freedom to develop differently. Especially with adopted children, who often want to fulfil their adoptive parents' expectations out of a sense of gratitude, this can lead to developmental problems. They can get the feeling that they have to be happy or successful to please their parents, while in fact they might not be willing or able to do so.

It is important that adoptive parents find the necessary balance between taking on their extra responsibility and providing the freedom necessary for their children to develop autonomously. It is also important that adoptive parents learn to accept that, just like any other parent, they will make mistakes, and that this is not something to be afraid of. It can even feel liberating for you, as well as for your child, to recognise that you are fallible. After all, everyone makes mistakes. It is a lot easier for a child to identify with a "human" parent who sometimes makes mistakes (just as he does), than with a parent who never makes mistakes or who at least never acknowledges this.

Adoption-related grief

The innumerable questions that adopted children have about their history and identity can evoke many complex and contradictory emotions. Those strong emotions are usually not the direct product of the adoption, but of the *pain of being given away*. (For a detailed evaluation of the concept of adoption-related grief, see Wolfs, 2008, Chapters 8 and 9). Because the sadness about this hurts a lot, teenagers may rather avoid this feeling. There is a chance that they will initially find themselves in a state of denial. After that, or simultaneously, they may start to look (perhaps unconsciously) for arguments to make their situation look better than it really is. Becoming angry can be another way to postpone dealing with sadness. Because of these (unconscious) strategies for evading pain, adopted teenagers in all their anger can start searching for the limits of their adoptive parents' love; without knowing it, they can be looking for the moment when they will be rejected once again. If the pain of being given away is not acknowledged in your child's evading strategies and behaviour, this can fuel his anger or denial and result in aggressive or even criminal behaviour. With some children, this anger will turn inwards, which may result in depression. Other children develop a fear of failure or a great sense of shame as a result of this unacknowledged pain; as a result of the abandonment, adopted teenagers are often convinced that they are not good.

If adopted children have developed sufficient basic trust and have the physical, cognitive and psychological disposition to develop healthily, they will experience a cycle of adoption-related feelings of grief during important developmental and life phases. The level of consciousness and the degree of intensity while passing through these cycles depend on many factors; their history, disposition and parenting situation are all very influential. Children also vary greatly in temperament; something that deeply wounds one might not even bruise another. Sisters and brothers from the same family often look back on their childhood very differently. In that sense, everyone experiences their history, disposition and parenting situation differently. But whatever the case, all internationally adopted children have been given up and have lost their parents and their roots. This history will somehow live on within them, and in this sense adoption is a fact of life that will be forever connected to their existence. Some need to connect with their past at a young age, while others might connect in adulthood, or later still.

So although there is a great variety in the ways that adopted teenagers grieve, it still seems that most teenagers start thinking about their adoption in a deeper way than they might have done before, and that the pain of being given up becomes more profound. Usually denial, anger or sadness about the relinquishment are healthy phases in an adoption-related process of grieving. However, if your teenager gets caught in a phase of grieving because the underlying pain is not recognised and acknowledged, anger especially can lead to problem behaviour. Kübler-Ross distinguishes five stages of grief (for a detailed description of these phases, see Wolfs, 2008, Chapter 8) that are experienced by adults as well as children if they 'grieve healthily':

- denial;
- reasoning/negotiating;
- anger;
- sadness/despair;
- detachment/understanding.

Every phase in the process is functional. Therefore, it is important that you recognise and verbalise the emotions that belong to each phase, so that your child feels acknowledged. As I described above, it depends on the individual child when they express feelings of loss and at what intensity. What is, however, consistent is that almost every adopted child passes through this cycle of feelings at important developmental moments in his life. Puberty is almost always such a moment of development. Themes that appear in this process of grieving are discussed in 'Additional topics for adopted teenagers'.

Although grieving is a process that everyone goes through in life, grief among adopted children varies greatly in certain aspects. Research in the field points out that loss through death is less damaging for children than loss through divorce or abandonment (Riley, 2005, p.62). Adoption corresponds to one of the two latter kinds of loss. There are several points where loss through adoption differs from "common loss":

- The loss is connected with voluntary renunciation and is felt as a rejection.
- There is no end to the loss and the rejection.
- The immediate cause of the situation is often unclear.
- Nothing is finite and information can change overnight.
- It is often not socially acceptable to be angry or sad about adoption.
- Society sees adoption as something positive. The child is provided with love and chances that he would not have been given otherwise. This notion of gratitude results in adopted children not daring to grieve openly at home.

For all these reasons, the process of grieving that adopted children go through can be quite complicated, tough and difficult. To be able to deal with the pain of adoption properly, they will need a lot of parental support. You may provide the necessary support by:

- helping your teenager develop basic trust;
- helping your child to recognise and accept his pain about being given up;
- recognising and dealing with your own experiences of loss or negative thoughts about yourself or the adoption. This will make you less inclined to let your behaviour/response patterns as a parent be influenced by unresolved or unacknowledged emotions. If both of you are aware of the pain that lies beneath certain thoughts or behaviour, the past will not exercise as many opposing forces;
- creating an open climate in which your teenager feels safe to talk about his adoption and heritage;
- being aware of the fact that the grieving process is the result of being relinquished, not the result of the adoption itself.

How you can actually support your child is dealt with thoroughly in Chapters 6–9.

If your child is given the chance to grieve and connect with his past, he will be less afraid of loss and better able to shape his relationships with others in the future. Loss, in the end, is a question of staying connected, not of letting go:

> Sometimes I wanted badly to find my mother, or perhaps talk to her once I would have found her, but sometimes I didn't at all. There were always feelings of doubt, fear and insecurity. Am I wise to dive into that realm and start digging, or not? Sometimes I would think about it for days, weeks or months; sometimes I didn't think about it at all. But the curiosity and emotions kept coming back. I'll carry these for my entire life, until I'm able to give them a place to rest. Maybe this will never happen. It's very hard for me to cope with all these thoughts and feelings. My husband, Marcel, also finds this very hard. I try to explain things to him, to engage him in what I do, but still I feel that he doesn't always understand. But it doesn't matter, as long as he lets me dig and burrow, supports me and listens to me.
> (Lijnie Siti Slamet, age 28, in Hoksbergen, 2006, p.102)

Conclusion: learning to recognise thoughts

In this chapter I have discussed the specific issues that adoptive families deal with in puberty. I have paused at adoption-related grief and the complex emotions that teenagers may experience as a result of their adoption history. To get a stronger grip on the complicated, adoption-related emotions of your child, in Chapters 3–5 I discuss the specific thoughts that can lie at the root of different emotions. Perhaps this will provide you with an insight into your teenager's realm of experience and the possibility of communicating more easily. The thoughts in these chapters are based on the section 'Additional topics for adopted teenagers'. In Chapter 6, I discuss the subjects that could play a role in your own experience of raising your teenager, based on the section 'Additional topics for parents'. In Chapters 7–9, I address the different communicative skills in depth. If you master a number of specific communication skills, chances are that you will be able to ask your teenager about adoption-related thoughts in a safe and open way, and be able to discuss them freely.

3

Identity, loyalty and the longing for roots

It is not enough for adopted children to know they are accepted by others. In the end, they will have to learn to accept and love themselves. Adopted children who manage to build up an identity are usually the ones who are provided with a chance to talk about their adoption in a satisfactory way within their family, and who receive help from their family in answering the question of how their adoption does or does not fit within their all inclusive self-awareness.
Daniel (age 20), adopted from Colombia

Inner conflicts as a result of identity formation

Like all teenagers, adopted teenagers start searching for their social and psychological identity during puberty (see 'Pre-adolescence (9–12 years): changes' and 'Puberty (12–18): changes' in Chapter 1). In doing so, they measure their self-image against that of their adoptive parents and the culture in which they live, as well as against that of their birth parents and the culture that they are genetically and historically connected to. They also form an identity based on the perceptions that friends and both sets of parents have of them. For most adopted teenagers, it is not easy to work through this process. In searching for information about themselves, they run into questions that, for the time being, cannot or can only partially be answered: 'Where do my talents, my temperament, my looks come from? In what ways do I resemble my birth parents? Why did they give me up? Was I wanted? Do they still think of me sometimes?' The search for answers to these questions is a complex task that can raise many paradoxical emotions. As a result of this healthy curiosity, adopted teenagers are confronted with another complicated issue: how to apportion their loyalties. On the one hand, they want to connect with their birth parents, but on the other hand they want to stay connected to their adoptive parents. If teenagers feel that either set of parents does not allow them to connect with the other, they can start experiencing a conflict of loyalty. This often leads to more paradoxical feelings and thoughts: 'I often think of my birth parents. I wonder how they are. Do my adoptive parents allow me to think of them? I yearn to get to know my birth parents, but I don't dare tell my parents.' If there is reason to think that the birth parents did not agree to giving up their child, the conflict of loyalties can be reversed: 'Am I allowed to love my adoptive parents? I don't think about my birth parents often enough. I feel guilty about that. They might really miss me, while I'm happy here. Is it OK for me to be happy and to love my adoptive parents?'

For adopted teenagers to be able to deal with these contradictory feelings and thoughts, they need a lot of basic trust and a safe environment at home where they feel free to talk about their birth parents and possibly to search for them. This will provide them with the best chance of building up a true and realistic identity. Inner conflicts will then block development as little as possible.

In this chapter, I discuss the most important ideas that adopted teenagers might have as a result of their developing identity. Along with every idea, I provide advice that might be helpful. At the end of this chapter, I give some advice on how to encourage openness, so that your teenager will be able to form her identity optimally.

I will never know who I really am

As I wrote earlier, teenagers need several kinds of information for the development of their identity. A part of their identity is formed by the situation at home, and by the image that their parents have of them. For example, you provide your child with a family structure, a set of norms and values, cultural and social heritage, financial status, a social environment, sexual role patterns, etc. You also provide your child with a self-image through the way you communicate with her. It is important that your child learns to incorporate your positive input into her identity during puberty, while she also learns to distinguish differences.

Another important part of her identity is formed at this stage by her peer group. This raises questions such as: 'Who do I want to belong with? Where do I feel at home? What body of ideas do I want to disseminate? What part of myself do I want to show? What is my sexual orientation? How do my friends see me?'

A third important part of teenagers' identity is formed by the genetic connection to their birth parents and the perception that those first parents have of them. Questions like 'Who do I resemble? What talents do I have, and who did I get them from? Do I have relatives (sister, brother, aunt, uncle, grandpa, grandma)? Why did they give me up? Was I wanted? Did they love me?' can only be answered if they have a genetic and historical knowledge of their past. Because adopted children often do not have this knowledge, they do not, or only partially, know themselves; therefore, to be able to form this part of their identity, they may start fantasising about their birth parents. These fantasies can get in the way of a healthy development, because they are often unrealistic. Too pretty a fantasy might cause your child to ignore your positive input. An image that is too negative will also result in lopsided development, because your child might miss the birth parents' input:

It felt to me as if I always thought more about who
I was and where I was from than others did. Whereas
that was only natural, because I really didn't know!
Yes, I knew that I was from Indonesia, yes, a small town
somewhere on Java. No pictures, no memories, no
family stories. I had to invent my own story. Find out
who I was, like any teenager. Except that I didn't have
to daydream about having been switched in hospital,
being a foundling, or fantasise about my parents not
really being my parents. They weren't. They were white
and I was brown. Not belonging was obvious enough
on the basis of outward appearance, it didn't leave
much for my childish imagination. So I dreamed on.
What my poor biological mother would look like.
Perhaps I had been switched in Indonesia, so that my
real mother was Megawati Sukarnopuri or something.
Not that she was in power at the time, I just frantically
fantasised about what my life might have been like in
Indonesia; shining shoes, working in a sweatshop,
selling my body, sick, weak, half dead. They were always
very sad fantasies, which made me happy to have
grown up in the Netherlands.
(Lijnie Siti Slamet, age 28, in Hoksbergen, 2006, p.98)

Advice: It is important that your adopted teenager develops a self-
image in which she incorporates both the positive and the more
negative sides of you and her birth parents. In this self-image, her
own strengths and weaknesses have to find a place. It is, therefore,
important that she feels free to talk and think about the genetic and
historical part of her identity, so that she can form an image that is
as realistic as possible.

It can help your teenager if she receives more information about her
birth parents during this period. It can also help if she learns more
about the circumstances surrounding her adoption, the home or
foster family she was in before the adoption, the place where she
was found, etc. It can also be to her advantage to learn how to

distinguish which characteristics she has inherited genetically and which characteristics, manners or points of view she has been taught by you and by the culture in which she is raised. This will help her to, in part, verbalise her genetic identity through introspection.

I want to meet my birth parents

As I wrote earlier, adopted teenagers often need more information about their history and their birth parents in order to get a better idea of who they are. Although children sometimes say they want to meet their birth parents, they often are not quite ready for it emotionally. Moreover, they often cannot foresee the consequences of such a meeting. In most cases, teenagers especially want to know about *genetic similarities*.

> I have always wondered if I resemble my biological mother, especially in the way I look. My sister (who was also adopted) and I used to say that we would like to be able to look at our parents from behind a one-way glass; from a safe distance and without having to interact. Perhaps some day I will try to find her, but I think it's essential that I know beforehand what it is I want to accomplish, and that it can also be a negative experience.
> (*Psychologiemagazine* webforum 'Als je geadopteerd bent', 18 October 2006)

Another important reason that adopted children want to meet their birth parents is to find out *why they were adopted*. The questions of whether they were wanted and whether the birth parents loved them are fundamental.

> Sometimes I think: they went through my birth, but afterwards they just did away with me. Then I feel as if I was thrown out, as if I am worthless. Sometimes it

makes me terribly angry. Perhaps it would help if I met them. I would so very much like to know if they loved me, and if they still think of me sometimes. Maybe they didn't just do away with me. Maybe they didn't have a choice. I would really like to know.

Advice: In many cases, meeting their birth parents is not the primary wish of adopted children, although it may seem that way at first. They want especially to learn more about themselves, so that they will be better able to shape their identity.

Look together for cultural events and gather information that will enable your teenager to identify with her background. Find out if it is possible to correspond with the birth parents (if they want to), the foster carers, the carers in the home your child stayed in, etc. Perhaps you can retrieve more information from them about the adoption by corresponding; perhaps they have memories of your child (or her parents) that they can put on paper for you. See if it is possible to get copies of police or hospital records. Those might have clues that might help you now or in the future. Discuss with your teenager what it is she wants to know, and what steps you can take. Keep in mind that your teenager might want to be intensely involved in this search one moment, while she drops her search at other times and might even think of it as unimportant. Let her know that you are willing to help, but that she can set her own pace. Let her know, too, that you will support her and assist her if she wants to make a trip to her birth country and really wants to try to find her roots.

Why did they leave me?

For adopted teenagers, it is important to know not only what their parents and friends think of them, but also what their birth parents think of them. In many cases this is unknown. Often, the only thing they know is that they were given up. Sometimes painful information is known about the circumstances your child was in before she was put up for adoption. Not knowing the reason why she was given up might lead to the formation of a negative self-image. Often, when adopted teenagers look for facts about the reason for adoption, they hope to find out that they were wanted and that their birth parents miss them.

> **I was extremely relieved to find out that my biological mother had not wanted to put me up for adoption. When I was born she was underage, and her family forced her to give up her baby for adoption. Now I knew that I was worth something! She had always prayed for me and hoped that we would meet again.**

Advice: Even if the reason for the adoption cannot be uncovered, or if the outcome is less positive, it is important for your teenager to know as much as possible about the reason for adoption. It is best to help your teenager gather as much information as possible about this. If all is well, you have already collected and discussed part of this information with her at a younger age; in puberty it is important that you deepen and extend that information if possible. This information may well be related to the political, social or cultural context of your child's native country. If she is allowed to feel sadness and anger about that situation and feels free to express these feelings of powerlessness to you, the chance of her being eventually able to partly accept the situation may grow. Her birth parents were, anyway, unable to provide for her; she was adopted because of the *situation*, not because she was unwanted *as a person*. If your teenager can learn to understand and accept this, she will probably be able to develop a more positive self-image (see also 'Why did they leave me?' in Chapter 4).

I want a child of my own

Adopted girls sometimes feel the urge to become pregnant at a very young age. Sometimes this is the result of the desire to better understand their own adoption. Through a pregnancy girls might, for example, wish to experience what their mother must have felt.

Wanting a pregnancy can also result from the need to feel a certain genetic connection and to be in a "self-evident" relationship that does not need fighting for:

> I was 19 when I started to feel the need to become a mother myself. I badly wanted to have children that were genetically related to me. In the end, I was 24 when my baby was born. I will never forget how they put my son on my tummy straight after his birth while we were still connected by the umbilical cord. From that first day on, I have been indissolubly connected to him. He is four now. He has my eyes and temperament; it is great to finally have someone with whom I feel genetically connected. Because however nice my adoptive parents were to me, I have missed that mirror my whole life. It may sound strange, but I can already enjoy the prospect of becoming a grandma someday!

Advice: Discuss the reason for your daughter's wish to have a child. Perhaps she strongly identifies with her birth mother and wants to mimic her by having a baby at an early age. Perhaps she wants to discover the feelings that her parents have had during pregnancy and after, so that she will better understand the reason for adoption (see 'Why did they leave me?' in Chapter 4). In both cases, it is important that your daughter learns to understand the nature of her desire. You can tell her that a pregnancy might provide answers to some important questions, but that it will also have lifelong consequences, which she is not quite able to foresee yet. A teenager's brain is not yet fully able to plan and anticipate, so it is important that you do this for her. Possibly you could find her a babysitting job so she can experience what it is like to care for children. In this way she will learn that raising and caring for children is a big, intensive task, and that it might be better to wait before having her own family. Discuss what other ways there are to find out more about her birth parents and the reason for adoption and actively do something with that. Create an open atmosphere at home in which your daughter feels safe to talk about her adoption.

Try to respond sensitively and responsively, so she can build a positive self-image in the here and now (see Chapter 7). This might make it possible for her to focus less on her birth parents as she develops her identity, and this may also make it possible for her to acknowledge her autonomous qualities and identify with her present environment (adoptive parents, friends, talents, etc).

If your teenager's wish to have a child springs from the desire to be genetically connected to someone, let her know that a child will definitely provide her with that connection, and that she is welcome to it, but that it is important that she does not engage in a close relationship too soon just because of this wish. Talk about the future together, and about the responsibilities and lifelong roles of parenthood. Your teenager may well be very independent in a variety of fields and quite capable of making decisions but her brain cannot foresee all the consequences of becoming a mother. As I wrote above, a teenager's brain often needs help in looking ahead, planning and organising and foreseeing the consequences of actions. At the same time, make sure to let her know that you will be very happy with a pregnancy once she is a young adult with the right partner, with whom she has thought her decision over carefully. Perhaps you can find another way to fulfil her desire until such time. Ask her what she feels is lacking and what it is she is longing for. Find out if it is possible for her to develop stronger roots. Maybe there is more information to be had about her past somewhere, or perhaps it will help her for now if she can identify with her native country in social, cultural or political ways. Perhaps she wants to make a trip to her birth country at the end of puberty to find out more about her roots, and maybe in the preceding years she could plan for this trip, either alone or with help from you.

I resemble my birth parents sexually

There is hardly a teenager who likes to think of her parents as sexually active creatures. That they have such a sexual identity is, however, obvious: the child's own existence is proof of that.

Although teenagers think that their sexual identity is formed by their peer group, it is often unconsciously derived from their parents too, who have been sexually active before the child's birth at least.

For adopted children this is more difficult. They do not owe their existence to their adoptive parents but to their birth parents. As a result of this, adopted teenagers may see their adoptive parents as asexual (possibly sterile) beings who have not been sexually active before their birth. In order to develop a sexual identity, they sometimes take only their birth parents as an example. If the birth parents have behaved irresponsibly during conception and/or during the time preceding the adoption, chances are that your teenager will measure herself against these standards. She may be convinced that she is destined for sexually irresponsible behaviour just like her birth parents. This feeling can possibly be intensified because she, like a lot of other teenagers, is suddenly experiencing heightened sexual and aggressive needs.

Advice: It is important for your teenager not to draw her sexual identity solely from her birth parents, but also from you. Let her know early on in puberty, or even before then, that your possible infertility does not mean you are sexually inactive. Adopted children unconsciously may think this. Show her in your daily life that you are not just parents, but husband and wife/partners too.

If your teenager behaves irresponsibly sexually, it is relevant to discuss this behaviour with her. Try to get her thoughts clear. Do not fill in things for her, but let her discover her own feelings and thoughts (see Chapters 8 and 9). Once your teenager understands where her behaviour stems from, she can learn that this behaviour is unnecessary because she lives in a different situation than her birth parents did. She may have inherited their temperament, but she can apply that same energy differently. Had her birth parents lived in different circumstances, it is likely that their decisions would have been different and their behaviour more responsible. At the same time, try to find as many answers as possible to questions surrounding the adoption, so that she will have the opportunity to build a balanced identity. Should your child remain excessively active sexually or persist in a wish to become pregnant at an early age, ask your adoption support worker for help.

I am a child of two worlds

On account of their history, but also because of their different ethnic and cultural background, internationally adopted children often already feel different at an early age. It is rare that they resemble their adoptive parents at all. Feeling different and, as a result, "not belonging" starts to play a part within her circle of friends too, as your child grows older. Especially in puberty, children want to belong with their friends. They want to be liked as they are, and develop a social identity this way. They also find support among friends on their road to adulthood; they find understanding about conflicts (for example, with parents), fears and uncertainties with each other. Adopted teenagers simultaneously feel the same as and different from their peers. Even just the fact that they are ethnically different makes it difficult for them to identify with their group of friends. Besides, they can only partially, or not at all, discuss their sadness, fear and anger about the adoption with peers, because for these children it is difficult to identify with a situation they do not know from experience.

Feeling different can mean a healthy challenge for teenagers, but it can also be hard, especially for these children who feel a strong need to belong to a group. They carry two cultures in one body. Lijnie Siti Slamet (age 28) writes about her teenage years:

> I wanted to speak Dutch as well as I could and I also just wanted to forget sometimes that I had a brown skin. I considered myself to be just another Dutch girl, with a slightly darker skin colour. Although it worked for me, the reality was, of course, that the rest of the world saw and still sees my outside appearance first: a small, brown Indonesian girl. I only recognised that when I

looked in the mirror. When I looked at my mother I saw a tall, Caucasian woman. I did not resemble her in any way. In secondary school, or at any school for that matter, I never really belonged. Sometimes I didn't want to. On the one hand I wanted to belong, like everyone else, but on the other hand I really didn't. I felt different from everyone else. Not special, but I couldn't and didn't want to follow the flock of sheep.
(in Hoksbergen, 2006, p.97)

When she walks around in her native country, Indonesia, as an adult woman with her young white husband ("orang belanda" in Indonesian), Lijnie Slamet writes:

[...] But as I'm walking there, through streets unknown to me, hearing a language that I do not understand, I'm overtaken by the feeling: I am at home. I feel it through bone and marrow, and it feels so good! The smells, the people, finally, everywhere I look: people who are like me. Here I am no longer the smallest, or the brownest, the odd one out.
(in Hoksbergen, 2006, p.97)

Advice: Besides your teenager being the same as others, you need to accept she is also different, and carries two cultures within her. If there are any indications that she has a hard time being different, talk about the differences that she experiences, not the similarities. Let her know that you love her regardless. Ask your teenager in what ways she feels connected to her native country. Perhaps she is interested in learning something or doing something that is part of her culture. Try to discover ways for her to express her difference – it is an integral part of her identity. Maybe she can contact other teenagers/adults from that same culture by taking language or cooking classes, dance lessons or music workshops, etc. If she is able to shape her ethnic identity more clearly, she may feel more balanced, and the sense that she has to identify 100 per cent with her British friends might diminish. Maybe your teenager needs to make contact with other adopted children. In that case, she might join an email group or contact other adopted children more often, either in her area or further afield.

My birth parents would probably understand me better

Almost all children, adopted or not, sometimes imagine having different parents who would understand them better, and with whom they would be happier. Carers, in the end, are not ideal human beings, in particular with respect to adolescents, who have the urge to confront them. Fantasising about other, more ideal parents, is an obvious thing to do, especially for children who have one or more parents whom they do not know (well). Teenagers whose parents have separated, for example, sometimes suddenly want to live with the other parent because they think this would solve confrontations at home. Adopted and foster children often feel the need to idealise "the other parent(s)", and because in many cases little is known about them, these fantasies can blow out of proportion. This can happen, for example, if they have developed insufficient basic trust or if their temperament clashes (temporarily or for an extended period of time) with that of their adoptive parents. A lack of realistic information can lead to a tendency to strongly idealise the birth parents.

Advice: Adopted and foster children often have negative associations with their birth parents. If they can connect to them in a positive way despite this, the development of their identity will be positively influenced. You can therefore confidently support such positive thoughts. If your teenager starts to idealise her birth parents too much, however, the development of her identity might be too restricted. In that case, it might be good to confront her with reality on occasion. You might want to say, for example:

> *Your parents would probably have loved to have raised you, and perhaps they would have done so very well. They probably do resemble you more than we do, and maybe*

you would have felt more at home with them. But they happened to be addicts, and they put you in dangerous situations. I don't know if your parents are still addicted, but there is a chance that they are. You can't get rid of an addiction easily. But, of course, I also hope that they are clean now. Perhaps someday you will be able to meet them.

Especially children who have been adopted at an older age can feel a strong, positive connection with their birth parents. They don't fantasise so much as harbour very lively memories of their parents or of other adults who were important to them at the time. It can be hard for you as an adoptive parent to accept and support this connection, especially if your child was abused in the past. It is, however, important that you accept this positive connection. It is likely that the grief over the past is too serious for your teenager and she embraces her birth parents in order to protect herself. Later on, when she is emotionally stronger and perhaps in therapy, she may be able to accept painful memories and process them. Try to react as sensitively and responsively as possible in each case (see Chapter 7) so that your teenager can develop a positive identity in the present too. Create an open atmosphere in which your teenager feels safe to talk about her birth parents and her feelings. This will enable her to feel loyal to her birth parents without feeling that this is forbidden, or that she is being rejected for it.

I long for my birth parents, but I don't dare to say so

Their wish to get to know their birth parents can make adopted teenagers feel insecure. They often want to remain loyal to their adoptive parents, who have taken care of them for a long time and who have removed them from a difficult situation in the past. All of a sudden they have this longing for "these other parents", which leads many adopted young people into an inner conflict: acknowledging their longing is often felt as a rejection of their adoptive parents.

> When I was angry, I used to yell at my mother that she had no right to tell me anything because she wasn't my real mother. This would make her feel insecure and I used to feel very guilty about it, afterwards. Perhaps this was just my way of acknowledging I had another mother, and that I was thinking about her. Sometimes I would imagine that I had been brought up by my real mother, and in those fantasies things were much more fun than they were at home. But then the next day I would feel guilty about that again. I would see my mother trying her best to make things pleasant and suddenly I would love her very much again.

Especially if your teenager has a strong sense of loyalty towards you, there is a chance that she does not feel comfortable talking about her fantasies and longings, and that she will quietly build up tensions that lead to inner conflict. Imagining a possible meeting can even arouse physical excitement resembling that of being in love, and your child may experience a strong sense of guilt about that.

Advice: If you are under the impression that your teenager is very busy with thoughts of her birth parents in silence, the best thing you can do is to give her some space. It is possible that she wants to get to know her own thoughts about this first, before she outwardly expresses them. Let your child know, as early on as possible, that she is always welcome to talk about her adoption and birth parents. Try to tentatively address these topics, or mention her birth parents in casual conversation.

> *Great that you made the team. You are so quick and agile, even as a little girl. I think you must have inherited that wonderful talent from your birth parents. Sometimes I try to imagine what they look like. They're probably just as athletic as you are.*

What a nasty row we had yesterday. We really do differ in temperament, I can see that. If I were you, I would be very curious about my birth parents, I think I would fantasise about them a lot. They probably resemble you a lot more than I do. If you ever want to talk about it, or want to find out more about them, I'd be glad to help. Just let me know.

You say you don't feel excluded by your friends, but you don't sound very happy when you talk about them. I can imagine that you feel different from the others sometimes because, after all, we are not your birth parents.

Tomorrow's your birthday. It's been 14 years since you were born. I often think about your birth mother around this time of the year. I am so happy that she brought you into this world, I enjoy your company so much! Do you think about her sometimes, or doesn't it concern you very much?

React as sensitively and responsively as possible (see Chapter 7), so that your teenager develops basic trust and a positive self-image. If she feels secure with you and feels she is a good person just as she is, she is likely to feel less obliged towards you and will speak more freely about her conflicting loyalties.

I am very happy with my adoptive parents and never think about the past

Some children carry their adoption history with them on a daily basis. Others would rather not think of it at all, even when they are adults.

Thirty years ago I was adopted by a loving Dutch couple. I never lacked anything. I still don't! I live my own legend and listen to my heart. That's how I became who I am today. A loving and warm person, without feelings of hatred. I am very grateful to my birth mother for providing me with the opportunity she has given me.

> The chance for a better life! A life that she could not provide. I have never suffered from attachment problems, something that is ascribed too often to adopted children, in my opinion. I can't even bear to think about the time when my adoptive parents won't be here any more. My heart goes out to them, with love and gratitude.
> (*Psychologiemagazine* webforum 'Als je geadopteerd bent', 'Ida', November 2006)

Most adopted children, however, do start thinking about their adoption at some time during their life – for example, when they become parents themselves, when they lose people dear to them, or when they reach milestones in their career.

> For a long time I thought my adoption did not have a large influence on my life. I always thought of my adoptive parents as my real parents. But when I thought about my adoption it would conjure up painful feelings that I couldn't handle very well: I would sooner hide them. When I had a child at 25, the grief over having been left suddenly hit so hard that I couldn't (or wouldn't) avoid it any longer. With the help of a psychotherapist I was able to deal with my adoption; the fact that I was adopted now has a great deal of influence on who I am! Many patterns, for example, my fear of rejection and feeling different, I can trace back to my adoption. The art is to let it work for you, but that is not always easy and I am sure that I will carry my adoption and its unpleasant side-effects with me for the rest of my life.
> (*Psychologiemagazine* webforum 'Als je geadopteerd bent', free from: 'Maggie', 18 October 2006)

The fact that your child is optimistic about her history at this moment may be the result of her nature, but also of the fact that it is too much of an emotional burden for her to be constantly aware of her history. Some children need a kind of "safety net" or even a family of their own before they can look back and address their history. By being very positive or casual, your child is able to keep the pain at a distance for a while.

Perhaps your teenager is especially loyal to you at this time of her life and thinks that she owes you her gratitude. That gratitude can take the form of unconditional love and showing you that you did well in adopting her (see above). Your child may also have developed a kind of "anti" attitude as a result of the many negative opinions that exist about adoption. This may lead her to feel the need to "prove the contrary" and let everyone know that many adopted children are very happy.

Advice: It can be healthy for your child not to want to think about her history temporarily. After all, there are many developmental tasks that a teenager needs to accomplish, and certainly not all of them are adoption related. It is, however, important that you recognise signals that may imply the contrary of what she says. She may say she does not think about her adoption, but then you notice she becomes more alert when the subject is mentioned indirectly, for example, in the media. Perhaps she says she is not concerned about her origins, but it turns out that her best friend is also from another ethnic background. You might say:

> *I know that you are not really thinking much about your adoption, but it is quite a coincidence that your best friend is Colombian too. Do you feel a stronger connection because of it, or doesn't it matter?*

Let your teenager know that she is free to bring up the subject if she wants, for example, by saying:

> *I could imagine that you sometimes think about your birth parents. If I were you I'd be rather curious about them. Don't hesitate to ask, if you ever have questions about the past.*

Make a connection with her birth country, celebrate the anniversary of her adoption or think up a ritual together that has to do with her native country. Do not deny differences, integrate them into your family life, without making your child feel that she should feel different. She can feel British perfectly well, and still have two cultural backgrounds. If you suspect that your teenager does not want to feel different out of loyalty to you, it is important that you let her know she can be loyal to two sets of parents, and that you do not feel rejected when she thinks about her native country or her birth parents (see above).

If your child reacts in an uncertain or evasive manner when you talk about her native country or the fact that she is different, you can ask for advice from an adoption support worker.

I feel guilty because I'm happy

When an adopted teenager feels happy in the family that she grows up in and does not think of her birth parents often, she may develop a feeling of guilt about this – especially if she suspects her birth parents gave her up involuntarily:

> I was perfectly happy and I almost never thought about my adoption. I was happy that my parents had given me up, because if I had grown up with them, I would have had far fewer opportunities. I felt at home in London and was happy with my adoptive parents and my friends. Still, there was always a sense of guilt bugging me underneath that happy feeling – because I was happy here and I hardly thought about my birth parents.

Advice: It is often hard to uncover the true feelings of teenagers. Your child may seem happy and securely connected within the family, but she may experience feelings of guilt at the same time. To provide your teenager with the space to talk about these

feelings, you could, for example, state your own feelings on the
subject:

> *You're such a wonderful girl. I see so often that you are*
> *having a good time. I really enjoy that. Sometimes I think*
> *about your birth parents. Wouldn't it be great if they knew*
> *what a wonderful time you're having? I know there's little*
> *sense in thinking about that; the chance is very small that*
> *you will ever meet. Perhaps you don't even want to, I could*
> *imagine that too. Meeting your parents can be very*
> *complicated and it can have a big impact. I could very well*
> *imagine that you don't want to search for them.*

Make it clear to her that she has a right not to look for her parents;
many adopted children decide not to in the end. Her parents gave
her up for adoption; she did not ask them to. That she was given up
is their responsibility; they wanted her to have a better future, and
that is what she got. Ultimately, that is what matters most. Let her
know that it's OK to enjoy the fact that she is happy now. Let her
know, too, that her needs may change in the future. There might
come a time when she does want to think about her adoption and
search for her birth parents.

My birth parents were horrible people, I was lucky to end up here

Perhaps your teenager's history is negative to such a degree that she
is unable to make a positive connection with her birth parents.
Possibly they abused her or abandoned her in a very traumatising
way. Maybe she roamed the streets and her parents did not care for
her at all. The pain this causes can be so intense that your teenager
only experiences feelings of anger and rejection.

Advice: In order to construct a healthy, appropriate identity your
teenager also needs to be connected to her birth parents in a
positive way. She is genetically related to them, so if she renounces

them, she essentially renounces herself. Her temperament, looks and talents stem directly from her birth parents. If your teenager has mostly negative memories, it is clear that she cannot connect to them positively. Before she can do so, it is necessary that she feels free to experience sadness and anger about what was done to her. Name and accept her sadness or anger (see also Chapter 7). Do not express your own opinion. If, in the future, she wants to make a positive comment, she shouldn't feel she can't because you feel differently. React in the most sensitive and responsive way possible; name the positive characteristics that she is likely to have inherited from her birth family – for example, her talents, amiable personality or attractive appearance. If your teenager builds up enough basic trust, there is a good chance that she will develop a positive self-image and, as a result, will be able to partially connect with her birth parents in a positive way.

Let your teenager know that her birth parents have certainly behaved badly, but that they might have behaved differently if their own circumstances had been different and more positive. People are shaped by their characters and also by their history and circumstances.

> *Your birth father hit you, and he never should have. Parents are not allowed to hit their children. But your father probably did not know how to deal with anger; chances are he never really learned how to. If you grow up in a poor, criminal neighbourhood, you learn to use your fists. Then, you don't realise that you can also resolve a fight by talking. If your birth father had been raised in a more prosperous neighbourhood and gone to a good school, just like you, then he would probably have learned that and he might not have hit you.*

If your teenager is caught in negative thinking, you might be able to help her by asking questions in a problem-solving way. I will go back to this in Chapter 9. If you suspect that she has, as a result of her history and/or aptitude, not been able to build up enough basic trust, it would be best to approach an adoption support worker.

Some more general advice

Your adopted teenager owes her existence to two pairs of parents. It is important that she can experience both relationships freely and openly. To allow herself to feel the lifelong connection with both sets of parents, it is important for her to build up enough basic trust and develop a positive self-image. On the basis of this trust, you will be able to build up a relationship together that is founded on reciprocity and respect. In order to achieve this goal, it is important that your child feels acknowledged by you. Reacting sensitively and responsively will improve the chances of your teenager feeling safe and secure enough at home to share her thoughts about her birth parents or her adoption. In Chapter 7, I will provide you with communication tools with which you can respond sensitively and responsively.

Make it clear to your teenager that she can freely relate to other people and that her relationship with you will not be destroyed or damaged if she does things differently from what you would like. In this context, family therapist Else-Marie van den Eerenbeemt uses the phrase 'freedom in togetherness' (2003, p.36). This interrelationship will give your teenager the ability to develop herself in a free and balanced way.

Adopted teenagers develop their identity on the basis of two sets of parents. If your teenager feels the need, you could help her along by summing up the characteristics that she has received through nature and through nurture. You can also look for characteristics that are unique in her. In what ways does she resemble her four parents? How is she different from them? How can I bring these things together? What makes me unique? In the appendix, I have listed several questions that might help your teenager to think about her identity or identities. The list is not complete, but it provides you with an idea of how she might define her identity.

If your teenager spends a lot of time considering a possible trip to her country of origin, you can best help her by making her thoughts on the subject more tangible. Why does she want to visit her native country; what does she want from such a trip? What does she expect to find? How does she think the trip will help her? Does she just want to visit her native country, or does she want to find her birth parents, too? Discuss the consequences of a possible trip or a meeting with her parents. What scenarios are possible, and is she prepared for all of them? Teenagers are capable of clear thought but their brains are not yet fully equipped for organising and planning ahead. Compose a questionnaire together. You might want to buy a special notepad or binder that she can use to write her questions and answers in. Perhaps when she is able to think about the consequences, she will come to the conclusion that she does not (yet) want to make the trip. Perhaps she merely wanted to fantasise about it out loud, and in doing so her needs may be fulfilled. If your teenager ultimately decides she wants to make a roots or culture tour to her birth country, you can best contact an adoption support worker and/or ask your adoption agency for advice about this.

4

Anger and aggression

Since adolescents rarely suffer in silence but often do not disclose the true source of their suffering, the result is often a furious, irritable and difficult young person.
Debbie Riley (2006, p.61)

Anger as a result of adoption

As a result of their history, adopted children often carry a great deal of anger with them. Frequently, beneath this anger lies *unprocessed grief* over having been given up by their birth parents. This pain often surfaces with great intensity during puberty, and can influence the child's self-image in a negative way: the deeper realisation that they were rejected by their first parents may cause them to feel they are worthless. This feeling can stand in the way of them attaining a realistic, balanced identity.

As a result of the pain over this initial rejection, some teenagers become grumpy and sombre, without knowing why they feel this way. The introverted, adopted Daniel (age 20) writes:

> My family displayed a rather cool response to my
> gloominess. Their average response amounted to as
> much as: 'Why Daniel, you're so often grumpy!' or, 'Try
> and do something active for a change.' In the
> meantime, I was unable to speak to anybody about my
> problems and feelings. Of course, at that time, I did not
> know how to explain my sentiments. All that time I
> spent alone in my room feeling dreadfully lonely. But I,
> too, didn't really know what was wrong with me.
> (in Hoksbergen, 2006, p.341)

Because of their feelings of grief, some teenagers test the
boundaries of their adoptive parents' love for them. Often the anger
is a result of the *compulsion to repeat*: they unconsciously search for
new rejection and confirmation that they are, indeed, "worthless".
Even a reprimand, or an angry or irritable response from the parent,
can be interpreted as a fundamental rejection. Adopted children can
also feel angry or helpless, because little is known about their birth
parents, because the reason for their adoption is unknown or very
hard to bear, or because they did not have any say over their destiny
as a young child.

Angry behaviour is mostly a healthy phase in processing adoption-
related grief (see 'Adoption-related grief' in Chapter 2). However, if
the underlying pain about relinquishment is not recognised, or if
your child has not been able to develop sufficient basic trust due to
his history, family circumstances or disposition, he might get stuck in
this angry phase. The anger will take on more serious proportions
and might result in problematic behaviour. Your teenager may start
acting aggressively or criminally, develop severe fear of failure or an
eating disorder, or become depressed. Cris da Silva (age 28) writes
the following about his adoption:

> Because of my adoption-related problems, and because
> I hung out with the wrong kind of boys and girls and,
> of course, because of my puberty, I kept ending up in
> the wrong circles. I did things that were completely

unacceptable. Until one day, when I was 18 years old, things truly got out of control and I ended up at the police station again (this had happened before when I was 15) for a couple of days. My parents were furious, but they still supported me and protected me, for which I am grateful to this day. For me it was a big blow, because I had always thought that something like that would not happen to me.

As I grew older, my life became increasingly intense. I got drawn into the criminal circuit deeper and deeper. I looked for this intentionally, because it was there that I felt accepted. To remain a popular guy, I was always at everybody's disposal. And so I had a lot of "friends". Nobody really knew what was going on behind the mask, however. How much sadness I carried with me about having been given up and how much I was thinking about my family in Brazil and how they were doing. Those issues comprised a large part of the problem. I had so many questions about myself: who I was, where I was from, why I had to be here, who my parents in Brazil actually were, and many more. (in Hoksbergen, 2006, pp.154–5)

In this chapter I map out the thoughts that may be at the heart of your teenager's sombre, angry or risky behaviour. Once you know what thoughts accompany which emotions, you are likely to understand him better and keep in closer contact with him. This may also enable your youngster to better understand where his anger comes from and (in the end) to reach the next phase in his grieving process. If he feels strong enough to experience the underlying emotions, he can connect with his roots and ultimately create a more realistic and balanced identity. In the last section of this chapter, I offer some general advice about how best to deal with your teenager's anger.

Why did they leave me?

In many cases the adopted child's anger springs from the fact that he cannot understand why his birth parents would have given him up. However well your teenager gets on with you, it often remains unthinkable for him that his birth parents gave him up for adoption. Adopted children often wonder if they were wanted children: 'Why was I given up? Wasn't I good enough? Was it my fault?'

Because an adopted teenager bases his social and psychological identity partially on the opinions that both sets of parents have of him, there is a strong need for a solid explanation: 'What did my birth mother feel when she gave me up? How has she felt since then? What does she think of the fact that she couldn't raise me? Is she sorry? Does she miss me? Why did she give me up when so many mothers in similar situations do not?'

> When I read the documents and go through my mother's reason for the adoption, it raises a lot of questions: who was she? What did she do for a living? Was her life too hard? Was she unable to raise me? Didn't she have the money? Was she forced to give me up? I feel confused, sad, because there aren't any answers to my many questions. At the same time I try to smooth these feelings and questions over somewhat and try to think of to what extent something like this is common. If perhaps it happens more often. My sister and I appear to have been born out of wedlock. Maybe we weren't really, but in those days this was the only passing reason for adoption. And the pregnant little line "for her to be of service to this country" in the adoption papers doesn't strike me as something that a simple farmer's girl would come up with for her baby daughter. Or maybe it does...
> (Lijnie Siti Slamet, age 28, in Hoksbergen, 2006, p.94)

If adopted teenagers do not receive answers to these questions, or receive only partial answers, and their parents do not recognise their pain, this may intensify their feelings of helplessness and anger. This anger may be aimed at the birth parents or at you (see below 'I do not feel at home here'), or at the institutions that do have information about your teenager but will not allow him access to it. If these questions are not answered satisfactorily, teenagers will find it difficult to grieve properly. Being desperate to find answers, some adopted young women will even long for early pregnancy, in order to closely approach the experience of biological parenthood. 'How did my birth mother feel? What kind of relationship did she have with me when I was still in her tummy? What went through her mind when she gave me up? Would I ever give up my child?' These are questions that they might be hoping to answer by becoming pregnant themselves (see also 'I want a child of my own' in Chapter 3). In an attempt to avoid thinking about these difficult questions, other adopted teenagers might wish to put off pregnancy for a long time. Sometimes pregnancy or birth can call up even more anger about having been abandoned. After the birth of her first child, the adopted Mirjam Hamoen (age 40) writes:

> I was unbelievably fond of my newborn baby daughter, Esther, but I did not know how to cope with this new primal feeling in me. I kept associating it with what Pam (my birth mother) must have felt. And I simply couldn't understand how she could ever have given up something as precious and beautiful as a child. A kind of rage began to come over me. The anger was directed at Pam, and I made that clear in all my letters to her. And still my anger kept growing.

> My emotions settled inside of me. I acquired a new drive that justified my actions. Again and again I would ask myself how in heaven's name she had been able to put me up for adoption. Me, who she had carried inside of her for nine months. Me, who she had felt inside her. Me, to whom she had given the gift of life. But I felt that I kept getting the wrong answers, which resulted

in my blaming my mother even more. In the end, Pam wisely stopped responding.

I set out to work through this process myself, with all the sadness, anger, helplessness and pain inside me. Letters to Pam that I never sent were a way of coping with my feelings. Paper always takes your side. That's what I needed. I was right, this was the way I felt. I had been rejected, I had been given up, I had been treated unjustly.
(in Hoksbergen, 2006, p.50)

Advice: Most adopted children want to know the reasons for their adoption because they need to know if they were wanted. Knowing if they were wanted or unwanted as a child can have a strong influence on the adopted child's self-image. If nothing, or only very little, is known about the adoption, there is a fair chance that your teenager will interpret the reasons behind it negatively. He might, for instance, experience a sense of powerlessness and become angry at the thought of having been given up just like that, and that no one has ever come up with a valid reason for it.

Try to accept your teenager's strong emotions about this and provide him with opportunities to express his feelings of helplessness. Most parents do not give up their children, not even under very difficult circumstances. Your teenager is entitled to feel angry. Act as sensitively and responsively as possible so your teenager can develop enough basic trust and a positive self-image (see Chapter 7). In developing a positive self-image at home, your teenager, might, in his identity-forming, focus less one-sidedly on his birth parents and what they might think of him. Give your teenager as much information as possible about the culture, traditions, and political and social situation in his native country. Perhaps this will help him to understand his birth parents' situation. It is very important for his identity formation to realise that he was given up due to the *situation* and not because he was not wanted *as a person* (see 'Why did they leave me?' in Chapter 3). If your teenager feels the need to have children of his own at a young age, try to discuss his underlying thoughts and emotions with him (see 'I want a child of my own' in Chapter 3).

Try to collect as many facts as possible about the situation surrounding his adoption. Discuss what institutions you might contact. Perhaps you could correspond with the orphanage, foster family or local child welfare institution. Maybe the adoption agency or aftercare organisation can provide you with clues. Do not keep secrets – tell your child everything that you know. Even if it is very painful information, your child needs this information to develop well. If you hesitate to give him certain facts because the information might be too painful, and you are afraid that your teenager might respond badly, contact an adoption support worker.

Why did you adopt me?

As I wrote above, the helpless feeling that your teenager experiences might turn against you. You took him from his birth country and he did not ask you to. His anger is aimed at the principles of adoption in general: if adoption had not been possible, he might still be living in his country of birth. However difficult his life might have been, he would at least have known all the facts and been aware of what his birth parents think of him. At certain times, it can seem more important for adopted children to know the facts and feel the genetic bond than to live in a wealthy country, be much loved and have a lot of opportunities for personal development.

> Whenever I see an ordinary family, I think, 'Why did I not get the chance to be with my own parents, my birth parents?' That just really hurts inside. I often try to talk with my parents about it. Or they try to talk about it to me. Often I simply cannot forgive them. I think, 'Do you realise how much pain you have caused me by adopting me?' They probably did it out of love. Something like:

'Her parents are probably very poor, we'll give her a
better future.' And I think that is a noble thing to do,
but on the other hand, it fills me with rage. There are
days when I think about it a lot, and feel utterly
worthless.
(Liora, in the documentary, *Zes adopties*, NCRV
Document, 2006)

Advice: Try to become engaged in your child's way of thinking.
How would you have felt if you had been taken away from your
parents at a young age? What would it be like for you if you had
no information about them, and if you did not know what they
thought of you? The anger that your child experiences is currently
directed at you, but it is very well possible that this resentment
will shift. At this moment, it is important for your child to know
you are aware of his pain and frustration. You could even decide
to express your own sensitivity on the subject; you may sometimes
feel doubt about whether or not you've done the right thing in
adopting him:

*We couldn't have children, but we did wish to raise a child.
We thought it would be a good thing to take you from
your hopeless situation, but as you are growing up, we see
how much suffering it's causing you, and we sometimes
doubt our decision. It was also selfish of us to want this.
But, on the other hand, you had so few chances for the
future, and your parents weren't able to raise you. I
understand that you are mad at us, but I want you to
know that we love you. When you are old enough, you
may want to visit your country of birth. I hope that this will
answer some of your questions. Perhaps we could start
looking for information that will help you to get started. If
you would like that, I would be happy to help you.*

My parents were bad people, so I am probably bad too

When your child reaches puberty, he will be affected by a major change in his hormonal levels. These will cause stronger sexual and aggressive feelings. As an adopted child, he may be more shocked by this than other young people are; he might not recognise himself any longer. His sudden, urgent needs may make him feel "genetically inferior" to you. Perhaps your teenager was molested or maybe his parents were addicted to drugs or depressed. In that case, he may start thinking that he has "inherited bad genes". If your teenager was born out of an incestuous relationship or a rape, he may project these thoughts onto himself.

Advice: Try to make it clear to your child that his birth parents may have acted in a way that seems wrong, but they possibly only did so because of their very difficult circumstances. Had they had other possibilities in their lives, they would probably have made different, more positive choices. If your teenager can see the connection between his birth parents' less desirable, or even irresponsible, behaviour and their living conditions, he may be able to appreciate that he is in a very different situation and can decide to make other, more positive choices. If you have better options, you can apply your genetic make-up differently, too:

> *You are afraid that you are as resentful as your father, and that you might behave just as badly as he did. But that does not have to be so. Your father probably never learned how to deal with those strong emotions. Do you remember how hard it was for you to learn to cope with your anger? But you now know how to cope with this differently. You can apply your anger to winning a football match, and that would make your entire team happy. If you like physical fights you can join a street gang, but you can also join the police or become a professional wrestler. It is very unfortunate that your father did not have those options.*

It is important for your teenager to see the human side of his parents. Whichever way you look at it, he is and always will be connected to them. It is much easier to cope with the idea that your father or mother was ill or lived under difficult circumstances, than it is to deal with the thought that he or she was a bad person.

I do not feel at home here

Your teenager may start having trouble identifying with you because of these stronger sexual and aggressive urges. Perhaps his temperament differs from yours and this could become magnified during this time of his stormy development.

If the differences in temperament and cognitive abilities are significant, this may confirm your teenager's idea that it would have been better if it hadn't been possible for him to be adopted. In accordance with this idea, he does not belong in this family or this culture. His angry, helpless feelings about this will probably be aimed mostly at you, because, as a parent, you are closest to him. Moreover, your presence confronts him with this irreversible situation on a daily basis. As a result, he may start to rebel against the neat and boring family he is living in.

This sense of "homelessness" may also be a result of your teenager's need for information. On the one hand, he wants to know more, but on the other hand, if he gets this information, he often seems unable to integrate this (new or old) information into his identity. Often, adopted teenagers must first go through intense emotions of grief, like anger or sadness (see 'Adoption-related grief' in Chapter 2). As writes Olvi van Repe (1975) who received her first photographs and a letter from her Indonesian family when she was 13:

> [...] The struggle within me and against myself keeps growing, because now I have faces to match the names. And yet they are only pictures. Is this really what I am looking for?

This has sparked off my rebellion against everything and everyone, my life in two worlds. These feelings make me feel very mutinous. Like at breakfast on Sundays. A weekly happening that I really dread. I prefer to eat by myself in my room, so I am sure to start a row with whoever is available in order to get sent to my room. That is my safe place. The time of 'intentionally looking for a conflict' has begun. I feel vulnerable, lonely and very misunderstood. I take offence at everything that is being said to me. Even when someone tells me that I'm the only creative one in the family, that makes me sad. Because I am the only one. I didn't get that from anyone around me. My brothers are good students, especially in maths and sciences. I am very bad at those and have to take extra classes. This, too, is an example of being unable to identify with the people around me. Still I try to find acknowledgment in the things I do. But when my mother tells me she loves me and that I have my own talents, I don't want to hear it. My two worlds are getting bigger. I am interested in Indonesia, but at the same time I am not.
(in Hoksbergen, 2006, p.19)

Advice: Accept your teenager's anger or despair. It is a result of his development. Your teenager needs to create a balanced, appropriate identity based on his heritage from *both* sets of parents. Provide him with as much information as possible, but be aware that this information may upset your teenager at first. If, at this moment, because of his development, your teenager mainly sees the things that set you apart, it is important for you to acknowledge these differences. Don't cover them up. Your teenager must learn to rebel against you and learn to connect with his birth parents. Let him know that you notice the differences, just like he does. Create a natural place for his original culture within your family. Accept his temperament and abilities. Name his feelings and behaviour often (see Chapter 7) so that he can develop a positive self-image in the present. Let him know that you love him for who he is, that he does not have to be like you, and that you will never leave him – not because he is different and not because he is angry. Chances are that he will develop more basic trust as a result of this, and that he will start to feel more at home with you (again). If it is clear that you respect him and that you won't abandon or reject him, he is likely to be more open to the similarities between you or to bonding with you. Create an open atmosphere in which your child feels safe to discuss his birth parents and his adoption.

If your child's anger does not subside, or if he starts to show signs of risky or delinquent behaviour as a result of this anger, contact an adoption support worker.

Others always decide for me – whatever I do, it's useless

In puberty, adopted children often start having more problems with the fact that others made decisions about their lives when they were very young. Now that they are becoming independent, they may feel a strong emotional need to take charge themselves. Having to adjust to their parents' rules in puberty could create more than average frustration, because of their history. Strict rules can cause them to feel that it is pointless to show any initiative because anything they come up with will be nipped in the bud. They can also be over-sensitive to situations of loss, which they have no control over – for example, when a friendship ends or when they break up with a girlfriend or boyfriend. Especially if they have not been able to develop enough basic trust due to their circumstances in life, their parenting situation or genetic disposition, they are likely to be unable to accept what has happened to them, even in the long term. As a result of this, they may behave oddly. In such cases, they often show their anger by acting negatively or aggressively, or by becoming extremely passive and showing less and less interest in school or other activities. Chances are that you will become concerned about his behaviour and will want to encourage and direct him more and more, leading to more extreme behaviour on his part.

Advice: It is important for your teenager to understand what is at the root of his feelings of helplessness and for him to know that it's OK to air his frustration. In this way, his anger will not turn inwards as much. Try to create an open climate in which he feels free to discuss his adoption. Try to react sensitively and responsively, so that he will be able to develop more basic trust; this is likely to lessen his need for strict control. Express your understanding of his feelings of helplessness and dependency. Ask him what things he would like more control over. Give him more responsibilities, but keep making sure he goes to school and gets enough rest and nutrition. Allow him a chance to show you that he can handle these responsibilities. Explain to him why it is necessary for him to abide by your rules sometimes. Make sure he knows that you have rules because you care about him. Draw up a plan together that makes him feel he is gradually gaining more control over his life. If your teenager is structurally caught in negative or passive behaviour, or if it seems he is incapable of carrying any responsibilities at all, ask an adoption support worker for advice.

I cannot please my adoptive parents

Sometimes the anger that adopted children feel is the result of the feeling that they have to conform too much to their adoptive parents' standards and expectations. Your teenager may feel he is not respected as a person. Perhaps he thinks he must always appear to be happy in order to please you, or that he should take on certain interests and values from you, while he does not feel any need to. Possibly he thinks he does not fit into your world because your temperaments are very different or because your interests are miles apart. If this is the case, his anger is likely to be aimed at you in particular, or at the social system that brought him to you. He could also direct his anger towards his birth parents, who did all this to him.

Advice: Try to provide your teenager with the space he needs in order to develop. Ask yourself: 'Do I have certain expectations of my child? What kind of expectations are they? Do they suit my child, or do they spring from my own needs? Do I expect my child to adjust himself to fit into our family style, and does that style actually suit him? Am I putting pressure on my child to be happy, while he may not be or not want to feel happy? Does he have enough space to be himself? Does he feel safe enough to talk about his adoption and birth parents? Are we paying enough attention to his culture and background?'

You might not be fully aware of the role your own past plays in your expectations of your child. Ask yourself: 'Can I truly see my child for who he is, or am I projecting my dreams and hopes onto him too much? Is it realistic to project my dream child onto him? Is it possible I am trying to prove a point to other families and to society as a whole, and do I expect too much of him as a result of that? Do I feel guilty about the adoption and is that why I want my child to be happy?' Your own projections can be treacherous pitfalls on the road to raising your child. I will elaborate on this in Chapter 6.

I'm always unlucky/people always abandon me

Sometimes adopted children have had the misfortune to experience separation or loss on more than one occasion at a young age. Perhaps you yourself have gone through a divorce, or perhaps several close relatives have died. Your teenager may have experienced loss more than once because he had to move house several times, or because several friendships have ended badly. If this has happened to him more than once, it is possible that he has become convinced that people will always leave him in the end anyway. His anger over what is constantly happening to him might be aimed at you or at his birth parents, who have given him this unfortunate life.

Advice: If your teenager has experienced several losses in the past, and has been unable to deal with them in a satisfactory way, his anger and rage over what was done to him may take on huge proportions. To be able to deal with the sadness about loss, it is important for your teenager to develop basic trust. Only then will he be able to experience the genuine pain behind his anger. Try to respond to him in a sensitive and responsive manner, and accept your teenager's anger (as much as possible). Explain to him that he has been very unfortunate in the past. If you yourself have played a role in this, for example, because you have been divorced or have had to move several times, do not deny your contribution to his anger. Try to explain your side of things, but also show him that you understand his anger. Remain supportive of him and assure him that his past misfortune does not predict a life of loss in the future. Try to make him see that what he has experienced is extremely complicated, and that it is almost impossible to deal with all of it on his own. Suggest to him that the pair of you find an adoption support worker who can help him, and let him know that you are willing to participate in the process. Adopted children who have experienced several losses in their young lives will often benefit from professional help.

How to deal with anger: general advice

(The advice in this section is based partially on Polderman, 2006.)

- Help your teenager learn to explain why he is angry and not bottle it up. Bottled-up anger will come out sooner or later – in most cases, in a more harmful and aggressive manner. Set an example to your child by not holding in your own feelings of anger, and by explaining immediately what has caused them.
- Teach your child and yourself that it is best to express your anger by mentioning your own feelings and needs (providing an "I"-message). Usually anger is directed outwards and onto others, which is hurtful and causes conflict. The underlying reason for the anger, however, is rooted in one's own needs. Accusations such as

'You never allow me anything!', follows from the need, 'I would so much like to have a bit more freedom'. Expressing your own feelings is not only a more honest way, but also a more constructive way of dealing with anger because there will be fewer reproaches.

- Be aware that aggression is often little more than self-criticism triggered by someone else. Your teenager's aggression is actually a sign that he does not accept himself (Delfos, 2005a).

- Show some understanding for your teenager's feelings of anger and disappointment, but do not accept rudeness or name-calling from him. If this happens, calmly end the conversation and let him know that you will be happy to continue at a later time when he is less upset. You cannot prohibit anger, but you can stop rude or disrespectful behaviour.

- If your teenager acts very angrily, it is best not to respond angrily yourself. There is a chance that the situation will get out of hand, or that you both retreat without having solved the problem. Try to figure out what is causing the anger and put it into words. Stay calm. Try to name the cause for the anger, not the anger itself, because that might make the situation escalate. If you can put the cause of his anger into words, your child will feel acknowledged. Moreover, in this way you will remain in control. Agree to address the subject again at a later time when your teenager has calmed down.

- If your own anger keeps resurfacing so strongly that you cannot suppress it, try to find out the reason for this. Perhaps you have difficulty dealing with anger as an emotion, or feel that you are falling short somehow and are frustrated about it. Perhaps you feel rejected because your teenager wants his life to be different from what you would like it to be. Possibly your anger is an expression of powerlessness, or you have bottled up your anger and are now blurting it out; your teenager's behaviour might be the proverbial final straw. Under all of these circumstances it can be difficult for you to allow your child to be angry and to accept his anger. Try to distinguish your teenager's fierce behaviour from your own emotions as much as possible.

- A real fit of anger is not your teenager's clever way to get your attention. It is a genuine basic need to give air to his suppressed emotions. This, however, does not imply that you should give in to your teenager's whims when he is throwing a tantrum (Hasselt-Mooy, 2002, p.64). If you give in to him, he will learn that it pays to get into a rage.

- Make sure that you keep the lead at home. If it is your child who decides the atmosphere in your home, this means you are losing control. Seriously losing your temper when your child is behaving badly is another sign that you are not in control. Young people feel most secure when there is a clear hierarchy in which the parents act as teachers or mentors. You are not the "boss", but you are the one who guides the conversations. Try to provide your teenager with a position of his own by verbalising his emotions and his behaviour frequently, by levelling with him and by treating him as an equal. Teenagers want to be seen and heard, and want to have the sense of "being somebody". This need can also be expressed in their excessive behaviour. By looking for solutions together and by frequently confirming that your are receiving his messages, your child will feel acknowledged as a human being; furthermore, this will automatically keep you in the leading position (see Chapter 7).

- Your teenager's behaviour can put enormous pressure on your relationship with your partner. You and your partner might respond quite differently, and this might lead to one parent becoming more strict as the other is becoming more indulgent. Teenagers will make use of this. Try to discuss this unevenness with your partner and decide on a course of action that suits you both. Divide up the roles if you have to: for example, one day you are the one that your teenager should talk to, the next day it's your partner he should address.

- Set up weekly or monthly family meetings in which the whole family is involved. What were the issues that you spoke about at the last meeting, what happened with them? What went well, what could have gone better? What things need attention? What issues on the agenda will be discussed next time? Also discuss the (family) rules and try to find a compromise, if necessary.

- If your child is angry often, try to make contact with him at a quiet moment. Try to get insight into his principal thoughts (see Chapter 9). Is his anger related to his adoption? Try to develop a plan of

action together. What are your teenager's thoughts on how to move
forward? What can you do to make this happen? Try to come to an
agreement about his (and possibly your own) angry behaviour. Make
it clear that you will accept his angry behaviour within certain
boundaries. Set up rules that you will both abide by. If you want to,
you could draw up a contract that you will all keep to.

- If your relationship has been seriously damaged, try to go back to
positive memories, to square one, together. Happy memories from
the past might bridge the gap and help you to give a fresh start to
your relationship. If both of you feel that the basis was a good one,
you may find an opening for the future. Your child will feel that
things were different between you in the past and that they may
change again in the future. It is very important for your teenager
that he does not only connect positively with his birth parents, but
also with you.

- Keep reassuring your teenager that you will not leave him, not even
when he gets extremely angry. Especially in this stormy period, it is
important for your adopted teenager to realise that he is in a secure
and consistent environment, with parents who will continue to
support him. However explosive the situation might become, do not
threaten to have him placed outside of your home or with any other
measures that imply you are rejecting him (by neglecting him, for
example, or by "letting him sort himself out"). Even though your
teenager behaves as if he wants to be rejected again, he is likely to
actually long for your unconditional loyalty and your indestructible
faith in him. If, however unfortunate, your teenager should be
placed outside of your home, reassure him of the fact that although
he is (temporarily) living elsewhere, he will always be your child, and
that you will do everything you can to keep in touch.

- Make sure that you do not let yourself get blown away by your
teenager. Now more than ever he needs basic rules and clarity. Your
teenager may want to be addressed as an adult, but he still cannot
foresee the consequences of his behaviour because his brain is not
yet fully developed. Recent research shows that the human brain
continues to develop until well after the 20th year of age. Compose
a (limited) list of basic rules together that your teenager has to stick
to, and give him some leeway in other areas. Your child will develop

further, his brain will mature more, and his hormones will peak less powerfully after around 16 or 17.

- If you want things to improve between yourself and your teenager, make a plan that also involves your own behaviour. Tell your child that you know that things will not change all at once, but that you would like to come to an agreement on one issue for now. Reward your teenager's improved behaviour verbally and pay minimal attention to moments of relapse. Your child knows very well what is expected of him, but cannot consistently behave according to your standards. By verbalising your appreciation of his positive behaviour, you improve chances of positive behaviour in the future. Also, verbally refer to your own behaviour. Say, for example, 'I got angry again yesterday, although I had promised I wouldn't. I also find it difficult to change my behaviour, but I'll keep trying.'

- Adopted teenagers often wonder if their adoptive parents really love them: 'How do they feel about me? Will they want to keep me with them?' Having an argument can be very scary if you are not sure of the other's loyalty. It may really help your teenager if you do not preach, but simply verbalise your own feelings. If you put your own fears and worries into words for your child and let him know how much you love him, this will help him to develop more basic trust and get to know you better as a person. Teenagers need honesty and reality very much. By speaking your own mind, your teenager will be able to connect with you in an honest way.

- Try not to linger on the lows in your relationship; teenagers can be extremely angry or selfish. While you may feel uneasy about a fight for days, your teenager may well forget about it within hours or a day. Do not take this personally, and continue to enjoy the good times. Keep looking for new ways to relate. Even if this doesn't improve the atmosphere immediately, your behaviour might have a positive effect in the long run. If your child notices that you are able to continue to put negative experiences behind you, he will gain more faith in you and in himself. In this case, your behaviour is an investment for the future.

- If your child frequently steals or lies, he is in fact screaming for your attention. Try not to lecture him or to think up doom-laden scenarios, but rather try and provide your child with good attention by reacting sensitively and responsively (see Chapter 7). Do not pay too much attention to negative behaviour itself, but put into words your thoughts on what you suppose might be the underlying causes of his behaviour.

- The emotional and cognitive development of adopted children do not always correspond. They may seem to be able to deal well with many things on a cognitive level, but their emotional development is much more challenged than that of children in genetically related families because of their adoption history. Experimental behaviour can be more risky for adopted teenagers (and for birth children without enough basic trust). If your teenager shows risk behaviour regularly, contact an adoption support worker and ask for advice.

- Keep in mind that puberty is a phase that will pass. Take your teenager's problems seriously, but also try to keep his behaviour in perspective and look beyond this period. Especially between 14 and 16 years of age, teenagers can react aggressively and exhibit risky behaviour. About this period, Martine Delfos says that 'parents should wait it out'. Chances are, that when your child looks back on this situation in years to come, he will be able to look at his fierce behaviour with more understanding and a broader perspective.

Rejection and abandonment, shame and guilt

*To me, adoption left me with an elementary feeling of insecurity.
I feel that I always have to prove I am good enough, that I am
worth loving. It is a result of the idea, 'I was once not good
enough'.*
Liliane Waanders ('Een kind blijft altijd bestaan', Trouw,
5 March 2007)

Fear, shame and guilt as a result of the adoption story

As I wrote in 'Adoption-related grief' in Chapter 2, most adopted
teenagers work through a complex process of grieving. If they have
developed enough basic trust and have the capacity to develop well,
they usually get through the various stages of this process relatively
unscathed. Some teenagers at first become infuriated by the
realisation that they have been given up and start looking for
boundaries to push that will lead to new abandonment (see Chapter
4). Some children will react in a way that is less extrovert; they may
turn their complex feelings about this first loss inwards. They might

become silent, fearful or depressed. However your teenager reacts, outwardly or inwardly, in most cases there are complex underlying feelings of fear, shame and guilt:

- fear of being left once more;
- shame about coming from a "bad family", or because her birth parents thought too little of her, and gave her up for that reason;
- guilt because she might not have been sweet and healthy enough as a child; she may feel this might be the reason she was given up.

In this chapter, I discuss the most important adoption-related thoughts that have to do with themes like rejection, abandonment, shame and guilt. It is only when thoughts and behaviour become conscious that the emotions behind them can be worked through. Then it will be possible to consciously choose new thoughts, feelings and behaviour.

It is better if I do not bond too much with people

Fear of bonding in adopted children is often the result of a fear of being abandoned. Making superficial contact is often not the problem, but making existing contacts deeper is. Lijnie Siti Slamet (age 28) writes about her teenage years:

> Making [superficial] contacts was not hard for me. [....] Since I'm afraid of being left by loved ones, I always try to keep a certain distance. In this way I try to protect myself from the possible pain that accompanies loss. When I was young, I suffered a lot from homesickness. I had difficulties staying overnight at a friend's – often I had to be picked up late at night by my parents. Maybe I was afraid of finding that no one was home when I got back, or I was afraid of missing things?
> (Hoksbergen, 2006, p.95)

Sometimes a certain amount of shame lies behind this fear of being abandoned. Olvi van Repe (age 31) writes about this:

> **Fear of bonding and fear of loss have always been major issues for me. Maybe they still are. My way of being really cool and independent about things is a self-defence mechanism. I don't want to give too much of myself away. Imagine that they find out who I really am. And what about bonding with someone? If that person tosses me aside, leaves me? What then?**
> **(Hoksbergen, 2006, p.23)**

The fear of being left again and/or the shame of showing your "real" self can be so great that adopted children suffer from it for the rest of their lives. Adopted children who have developed too little basic trust, or who have not had enough chances to grieve over being given up, are especially at risk of not being able to bond (any more).

Advice: Losses must be processed. Only when the anger, the rage and/or the sadness about a loss have been experienced fully, will someone be able to reconcile the past with the present. Provide your teenager with the space to process her loss and respect her feelings.

Respect the amount of time that she will need to deal with these feelings. React as sensitively and responsively as possible and let her know that she is fine the way she is, that you love her very much, even when she is angry or sad. In this way, she will be able to gain (more) basic trust and develop a positive self-image. Try to map out not only negative but also positive connections with her past, for example, by trying to show her the qualities and talents that she has. Only when your teenager has a positive self-image and dares to start connecting with the good parts of her birth family will she be able to love herself and (thereby) others. Moreover, her extreme fear of abandonment will lessen, because during the process of grieving she will also have learned to feel that she is worthwhile.

My parents want me to become independent, they will probably be happy when I leave home

During puberty, your child is preparing herself for an independent life without you. If all is well, she will be able to function independently by the end of this period. Although this is an exciting and challenging process, it also leaves an adopted teenager in a very vulnerable position. The process of letting go in particular makes her especially sensitive to rejection and abandonment.

> During puberty my parents encouraged me to become independent. They gave me a lot of freedom. For example, I was allowed to make up my own mind about what time to come home after a night on the town. On the one hand, I thought that was very cool and I could be proud of the freedom that I had gained. On the other hand, I blamed my parents for it. Why did they let me go? They probably wanted me to be gone as soon as possible. I could get angry at them about the silliest things at that time.

While you might be doing your best to allow your child to take on responsibilities and slowly let your role as a parent go, your teenager may interpret this sign in the wrong way. She might conclude that you want her to become independent as soon as possible *so that you will be rid of her*.

Children who have not been able to build up sufficient basic trust, for example, because of their genetic predisposition or a complex history, can be especially sensitive to this idea. Also, children who have an oppositional or spirited temperament and who seek confrontations all the time, or children who have a strong feeling of not belonging in this family, might feel insecure in this process of becoming independent.

Advice: Provide your teenager with extra trust in this phase by reacting sensitively and responsively (see Chapter 7). Behave positively and show her often that you like having her around. Let her know that every teenager sometimes seeks confrontations, that this is part of growing up and that you accept it. Perhaps you were once a troublesome teenager yourself; you might want to refer to this. Discuss the process of growing up. Teenagers cannot yet really comprehend the future and it might help your teenager if you show her the road to independence. Ask her what she thinks about becoming independent. Talk about the fact that you are giving her more freedom. Does she think it is pleasant? Explain that you are not giving her this freedom because you want to lose her, but because you want her to become a responsible, independent adult. Let her know that you enjoy having her at home, but also let her know that you will like it when you are both adults. Fantasise together about what it will be like when she is a grown-up – how often you will see each other, what you will do. In particular, let your teenager know that you will not abandon her, even if it might seem that way right now.

If I am too rebellious, I will lose my adoptive parents

Young children want to please their parents and follow their parents' rules. Usually they still idealise their parents. But in puberty, children start seeing their parents' (often exaggerated) imperfections. Adolescents look for their ideals in pop stars, celebrities, aunts/uncles, mentors, etc. Adopted children sometimes do not dare to rebel against their parents in a healthy way. They are afraid of losing yet another set of parents. They sometimes have the feeling that they have to be grateful because you have provided them with a better life, even if you have told your child time and again that this is not necessary. They might also feel uncomfortable with their adolescent friends, who often complain endlessly about their parents. A result may be that your teenager starts displaying socially acceptable behaviour and seemingly passes through puberty with no problems at all. Her desirable behaviour is possibly the result of her fear of being rejected again if she doesn't live up to your expectations. Mirjam Hamoen (age 40) writes about her youth:

> [...] I did not understand [my adopted brother] Job. I
> was also afraid of him. But I was even more afraid that
> he would be sent away because of his behaviour. That
> was my great fear, who can tell me that I can stay,
> when deep in your heart you know that your own
> mother has "given you up", although you were only a
> bundle of innocence? That uncertainty really ate away
> at me. I adopted a second nature, adjusting to my
> surroundings. In this way I created the feeling for
> myself that I was sure to be able to stay. So I was always
> adjusting to what my mother wanted, looking for ways
> to please her.
> (Hoksbergen, 2006, p.43)

Advice: React as sensitively and responsively as possible, so your
teenager will be able to build up enough basic trust and a positive
self-image. If she has a positive self-image and feels accepted by
you, she will dare to show more of herself and will be less afraid of
being left by you if she is angry or rebellious. If necessary, talk about
the adoption. You could use an interview or an article in the
newspaper as a way of starting the conversation, or you could use
examples from other adoptive families. Let her know that a lot of
adopted children experience a fear of loss and abandonment. Tell
her why, so she will be able to understand her feelings and put
them in perspective.

If I leave home, I will be alone again

Living on your own can be a wonderful experience, but it also
carries a loss, namely the loss of the warmth and security of the
family and the well-known home. Adopted children are often
(consciously or unconsciously) more sensitive to this situation,
because they have already gone through a very big experience of
loss in their life. Therefore they may have more problems with the
idea of leaving home some day. Some adopted teenagers even hate
the idea of having to leave home so badly that they take the

decision too early, out of fear. It may seem as if your child has chosen freely to leave, but that may not be the case. In most cases, however, it is the other way around. Children who are sensitive to loss will be tempted to postpone the idea of living on their own.

> I did not understand my friends, who wanted nothing more than to stand on their own two feet. I had it fine at home; my mother was a terrific cook and we were always chatting happily. I did not recognise that I was in fact holding on to that happiness out of a sheer terror of leaving home. Only when it was actually happening, did the idea hit me – I had not seen it coming. There we were, in front of my new home: my mother kissed me and walked away. Suddenly, I saw myself as a toddler, while my mother turned away and left me forever. There was no solid ground under my feet any more.

Advice: Bring up living alone occasionally. Try saying things like:

> *In a while you will be living on your own. I can imagine that you are excited about that. I know I was, long ago.*

Or:

> *Now it seems that you like the idea of living on your own. We really appreciate that. When the time comes, we will all help you move. But that feeling of happiness may change, that is possible. I remember that I really wanted to leave home, just like you. But when I was finally there, and my mother drove off and I was alone in my new room, that was pretty awkward. It took me a while to adjust to the idea that she wasn't there every day. If you feel that way, will you let me know? You can start off living at home half of the time, if you would like. And if you'd prefer to wait, that's fine too. As long as you follow your heart, it will be alright.*

Convince your teenager that your relationship will not come to
an end and that you will be there when she needs you. It is not
necessary to live in the same house in order to still feel a strong
connection. In some cases, the attachment becomes even more
intense. When you feel connected to other people in your heart,
you never need feel lonely.

Try to fantasise about what your relationship will be like in the
future – perhaps you can call each other daily, or use email or
Facebook to keep in touch. Perhaps your teenager has her own
ideas about how to keep in touch with you. She might want to
come home every weekend. Think about what you would like to
do together. Ask her what she thinks her days will be like. Make the
situation somewhat more tangible; that will probably make a lot of
uncertainty disappear. Explain that grandma and grandpa are still
your parents too and that they will always be. Be certain that your
child understands that you will miss her very much, but that you are
also excited about developing a new, grown-up relationship.

If you have plans of moving after your child leaves home, try to
suspend these plans so she will be able to come home for a while
to her familiar environment. If you are forced to leave because of
unforeseen circumstances, let her know that the new house will also
be her home. Perhaps you can make her a place of her own with
her old stuff. It is important that your teenager understands that
moving house does not mean that you are moving away from her.

I should not have existed

Adopted children and foster children, but also children with
separated parents, sometimes doubt their right to exist.

> My parents divorced when I was twenty. My father
> turned out to be gay and suddenly had a boyfriend. I
> was very upset. Not really because my parents didn't
> live together, but because the reasons for my existence

> seemed to crumble: if my father was really gay, he must
> have been when he married my mother. I felt that their
> relationship was based on a lie and that I really
> shouldn't have existed.

For adopted children, it is not only that they doubt their right to
exist, but also, as a result of this, that they have been completely cut
off from their roots. The conviction that 'I really should never have
existed' can in this way deeply affect their self-esteem. Mirjam
Hamoen (age 40) writes, after having gone into therapy as an adult:

> [My therapist], having given me all her love and
> knowledge, really pushed me in the right direction.
> My wound became tangible; I started realising that my
> bitter roots had their origin in the feeling that I had no
> right to exist. But those roots in my soul knew many
> branches. I had reacted to the feelings and wounds that
> affected my soul and in this way I spun a web of lies.
> Unconsciously I had set myself many rules and
> prohibitions. 'I was not allowed to be here', 'I was not
> allowed to be happy', 'I was not allowed to be funny,
> or to be sad' – and I can go on and on listing more
> prohibitions.
> (Hoksbergen, 2006, pp.54–5)

Advice: Accept that these feelings exist and that it is hard for your
teenager to give them a place in her life. React sensitively and
responsively (see Chapter 7) so that your teenager will feel she is
seen and heard. If you acknowledge her pain, she will at least
experience the space necessary for working through her sadness or
frustration. The recognition of this sadness can give her the feeling
that you see her. Try (as far as possible) to explain the context of her
conception and birth as they probably took place. Try to make room
for positive aspects, so your teenager can also positively connect
with her birth. You might want to say:

Your father and mother did not love each other. They
probably thought that was "normal". Perhaps they had
never learned how it feels to love someone. If a child does
not learn such things, then it is very hard to acquire
knowledge of this as a grown-up. They slept with each
other and you were conceived. After that, your father left
your mother. Luckily, something very beautiful came from
their relationship: you were born. I think your mother
found it very hard to let you go as a baby. Because,
although she had never learned to love anyone, you were
her child anyway.

You can help your child create a different story and associate new
images with the beginnings of her existence through the use of a
problem-solving questioning method. I will describe this in Chapter 9.

I have to show that I have a right to be here

Many adopted children have the feeling that they have to prove
their right to exist to everything and everyone around them and that
they have to show that their lives are meaningful.

'I will always behave nicely, otherwise you might
send me back.' At age six, I wrote this sort of note to
my adoptive parents. It has been the thread that runs
through my life; I always have to prove myself to
everything and to everyone. I must prove to myself
that I have a right to be here, that my life is of use
somehow, that my mother did not give me up for
nothing. In the adoption papers it says, literally, that
I was given up 'so that I would be able to make
something out of my life and could contribute to
society'. When I read that for the first time, it really
struck me. It has always stuck in my head unconsciously.
The urge to show that I am worth something, that I
took that chance with open arms. It is a mission that I

set myself, but that can also make me impatient with other people. Life has so much to offer and most people let those offers go by. That is incomprehensible to me. (Lijnie Siti Slamet, age 28, in Hoksbergen, 2006, p.98)

Advice: If your teenager has a great urge to accomplish things, nothing is really wrong with that. Her urge to accomplish things can do her lots of good in life. However, it is also a good thing to learn to relax. Try to find out if her drive to achieve is the result of her adoption. Perhaps she is always so eager to achieve because she fears that she isn't good enough. Let your child know that she is fine just the way she is and that you will also love her if she fails a test, or if she is not always the best or the sweetest. Try to react sensitively and responsively. If your child feels that she is seen, she may have less of an urge to prove herself. You can also try talking about it by means of a comparison.

I read this really interesting interview with an adopted child last week. It was about a young Ethiopian woman who had been adopted at the age of two by an English family. In the interview, she says that she always feels the need to prove herself and that she wants to show how good she is. Somehow it made me think of you; this woman was like you in many ways. If you'd like, I could let you read it sometime.

It is my fault that I was given up

Children easily blame themselves for their parents' behaviour. Adopted children and foster children ask themselves once again, during puberty, why they were adopted. Because your teenager is vulnerable during this period anyway, the (presumable) answer to this question may make them even more insecure. Why did her birth parents reject her? Why did they beat her? Did they not want her because she is ugly? Or because something is wrong with her? Was she not nice enough to them? Why did they not put her up

temporarily with an aunt or a sweet grandma? Some children
(Chinese girls, for example) may blame themselves for being the
wrong sex. Whatever questions your child may ask out of feelings
of guilt, her conclusion might in the end be that she was responsible
for being given up.

Advice: Talk to your teenager about her feelings of shame and
about the reasons why she was given up: What thoughts does she
have, exactly? What does she feel responsible for? Let her think
actively about these feelings of guilt. Perhaps she herself can think
of ways to get rid of them. If she does not come up with any good
ways after a while, you may want to come up with suggestions
yourself.

Provide her with as much information as possible about the situation
of her adoption and/or the political or social reasons for the
adoption. If your teenager knows as much as possible about the
context of her adoption, she will be better able to understand that
she was only a baby (sometimes not even born yet), and that she
cannot possibly be held responsible for what happened. Besides
that, if she gets to know the situation in her birth country, she can
gain more insight into the structure of her family, its poverty, its
manners, its cultural and its political morale. She might be better
able to understand the situation of her birth parents. By making the
adoption story as tangible as possible, she may start to see that her
feelings of guilt are pointless.

I am worthless

Many adopted children are ashamed of the situation that they were
found in, or of the family situation that was the reason for their
adoption. They can be convinced that for this reason they are not
worth anything and that others do not think highly of them either.
Your child may also feel ashamed because she feels rejected or
thrown out. The 18-year-old Liora says in a documentary:

I was five days old when I was given up. Therefore I
do not know my birth parents. I have had a lot of
problems, and I sometimes still do. You just do things
without thinking. Start taking drugs or hanging around
in the streets with the wrong crowds, that influence you
negatively. You start thinking: Yeah, they gave birth to
me. And then they gave me up and now I'm here. And
now I've got the problems here. You just feel worthless
then. I have the feeling that I'm constantly being passed
around, like: Oh, you take her. She isn't worth much to
us, anyway. You take her.
(*Zes adopties*, NCRV Document, 2006)

Advice: It is important for children to be able to show their feelings
of shame. Only when they have been verbalised and acknowledged
is there a chance to let in other thoughts. If, for example, the birth
parents have left their child somewhere as a foundling, that does
not say much about whether they loved their child or not. No parent
just gives up her child. Sometimes parents are forced to do so by
politics or by their culture, or because of their personal
circumstances. In most cases, the parents think of their child just as
often as the child thinks of them. If your teenager is ashamed of the
unfortunate circumstances that her birth family was in, you can best
explain to her that people are also influenced by the situation in
which they are raised and the situation they grow up in. Try to
explain:

*Your parents would probably have been different people
if they had been richer, or had grown up in a different
country. In some countries, people who are poor do not
even have the opportunity to go to school. In most
Western countries, the governments pay for school, and all
children are expected to go to school. That's how you learn
a lot as a child, that's normal. But your parents weren't
able to learn as much, not from their parents and not from
their teachers at school. Maybe that's why they didn't
know how to live a better life. If they had had different*

*examples from their parents, or if they had had more
money or had lived in a country with different political
or economic conditions, maybe they would have been
different people and they would probably not have given
you up.*

If your child was abandoned as a foundling, you could explain why
the parents might have done this and why they did not bring the
child to a home. In one country, parents might be risking a prison
sentence; in another country, the parents might be rejected by their
family. Try to help your teenager understand the circumstances in
which her parents were forced to make this decision, and how hard
they presumably found it. If she is able to understand this, she may
see that she was given up because of a difficult situation and not
because she was worthless as a person. Possibly she will then feel
less "thrown away".

Maybe your child will react angrily if you describe the difficult
situation that her birth parents might have been in. There are, in the
end, lots of parents in similar situations who do not even think of
abandoning their children. In the end, most children are not given
up. Although your teenager has to learn to live with the knowledge
that her parents did give her up, it can help her if you are aware of
and accept her anger and indignation.

My adoptive parents would have wanted their own child; if that had happened, they would never have adopted me

Adopted children can have the feeling 'that they shouldn't have been
here' (also see 'I should not have existed' above). This feeling can be
strengthened by the fact that they were "second choice" in their
adoptive family too. If you had been able to have children of your
own, most adoptive parents would probably never have adopted.
This pain can have a negative effect on the self-image of your child.

Of course I understand that my family meant well. They wanted to help a little child in need. Very nice. But that idea only arose after they had realised that they could not have children of their own. If they had become pregnant 'in the ordinary way', I would never have been here. That really bugs me sometimes. My birth mother didn't want me, but my adoptive parents didn't really either. Of course I know they love me, still I feel like a second choice sometimes.

Advice: Accept that your teenager feels this pain. The chances are that she would not have been with you if you had been able to have your own child. However, in the end it will not help your teenager to keep repeating these thoughts. It also won't help if you develop a feeling of guilt about this. Try to get your teenager to look at the situation from a different perspective; in the eyes of many adopted adults there are essential positive sides to the egoistic child-wish of unwanted childless parents.

Of course it is strange in the beginning of your life, if your mother doesn't want you. Of course you think about that. But this also has other sides – in my case I instead got a mother and a father who really became my mother and father. Who wanted children and couldn't have them, yes. Thank god they wanted children! Imagine ending up with parents who really didn't want you, but only adopted you because they wanted to save the world.
(Stephan Sanders in NRC, 'Opgevangen of ontvoerd, geadopteerden ageren tegen hun adoptie', 30 December 2006)

and:

My parents very much wanted children, but after ten years of marriage my mother had still not become pregnant. That is why they wanted to try to adopt a child. They were extremely happy when they heard that they would be allowed to adopt me and have always shown that happiness since. That is so incredibly important, feeling valued as a child. I am convinced that, as a result of their happiness, I accepted my adoption fairly easily. If my parents hadn't given me the feeling that I am very important to them, I would probably have started to doubt myself. In the end I was given up by my biological parents and that can hurt your self-esteem very easily. But I never felt lonely or unhappy because throughout my youth I was surrounded by warmth.

(Everdien Francken, age 30, in 'Geadopteerd en nu zelf een kindje, hoe beleef je dan het moederschap?', *Vriendin nr. 38*, September 2004)

Perhaps you can start a philosophical conversation with your teenager about the realisation of dreams. Possibly you could help her to realise that almost all people have seen dreams shattered, but that doesn't mean you stop dreaming. You could, for example, start the conversation with the following question: 'What would you do if the man of your dreams left you just before your wedding? Do you think you would ever be happy again?' Tell your child that people can always give themselves new chances – and people who dare to do that can realise many dreams in their lives. Sometimes those dreams may even turn out to be more beautiful than the first dream. Feel free to show your own grief about the fact that you weren't able to have children, but be sure to demonstrate how happy you are that your child came into your life. Let her know that you love her for who she is, and that you would never exchange her for a birth child. Let her know that you do not expect her to 'be like you', or 'have the same dreams as you'. The fact that you realised your own dream by adopting her, must not lead her to the thought that she has to be grateful.

A child of their own would probably have made my adoptive parents happier

Children are by nature inclined to give. They are often out to please their parents. If their parents are unhappy, and if in some period of time contact with them is difficult, the children may start to think that this is their fault. Children of divorced parents sometimes are convinced that the divorce is the result of their behaviour.

Adopted and foster children sometimes feel guilty too, especially if they differ greatly from their parents. If your adopted teenager's temperament starts to collide with yours during puberty, this may be a reason for her to think that 'you would have been happier with a birth child'. Possibly you will catch yourself thinking sometimes that you and a birth child might have looked more like each other and possibly would have had a stronger bond (see Chapter 6).

Advice: Let your teenager know that you love her, despite her behaviour. Try to get her to express her insecure thoughts. You could, for example, do this by verbalising your own thoughts or trying something like this:

> *We have been fighting a lot, lately. Of course that's not enjoyable but it is a part of puberty. And of course we are not very much alike. Sometimes I feel really sad that we are so unalike. On the other hand, I really like it because it helps me see other people from a completely different perspective. And of course I learn a lot about myself too. That I am pretty boring, for example. It must be really hard for you sometimes, that we're so different. (Or does that not really bother you?)*

Talk about the past, about memories and about times that you were really close. Think about your first meeting in the country of your child's birth. Let your teenager know how much you wanted her and how you enjoyed her when she was little. These positive memories may be able to tighten your bond and give your teenager the feeling that she once did make you happy. Make it clear to her that you are sensitive to the fact that she is now in a turbulent phase of life and assure her that, in a while, things will possibly calm down a bit. If necessary, investigate your own drives and uncertainties about your unwanted childlessness (see Chapter 6). These feelings can become even stronger when your child is going through puberty. Accept that these feelings exist; tell your teenager that you once had the intense desire to have your own birth child, but that you wanted to have her just as much. You might want to show examples of genetically-related families who do not resemble each other at all. In the end, it is completely uncertain whether or not a child of your own would have resembled you.

I feel like a misfit

Adopted children feel different for several reasons – because of their history and their different appearance, interests or temperament. Sometimes these thoughts are fed by the fact that they do not genetically resemble their parents or siblings. Especially if parents are more attentive to the similarities than the differences, it is possible for adopted children to get the feeling that they are not seen and accepted. Sometimes adopted children feel different because they make trouble in school or at home, perhaps more than other children within or outside the family. They can become convinced that there is something wrong with them. Daniel (age 20), adopted from Colombia, writes:

> I often feel mad because I am the only one with so many problems and I feel sad because I've got the feeling that it won't change. I'd also rather do more fun stuff than working out these problems all the time. Why couldn't I [as a teenager] do just as well as the others? I unconsciously blamed myself. Something was wrong and I was weird and different. [I thought that] if only I would try harder to be like the rest,

everything would turn out right.
(Hoksbergen, 2006, p.341)

Adopted children like Daniel who grow up in a mixed family can be even more susceptible to the feeling of being different. Especially if the other children have fewer problems and/or are more like their parents. Although you might not make distinctions between your children and you love them all equally, it can still be hard for your teenager to deal with these differences. In the end, he does differ genetically, ethnically and culturally from the rest of the family. Daniel writes the following about the mixed family he was raised in:

> My parents have three biological children and I have always felt that I just did not fit in as much as they did. Sometimes I would articulate this and the reaction would usually be: 'Daniël, of course you are a part of the family!' This was all meant well, but somehow I only felt worse when I heard it. One point where we have certainly differed is in making social contacts. My brother and sisters felt a lot more free and relaxed in making friends. I have always found that difficult and felt inferior because of just that. I see how my parents enjoy the friendships and intimate relationships that the other children have. My introvert and lonely existence has always stood very much in contrast to that. I have always thought that I must have some sort of birth defect, which makes me different from everyone else.
> (in Hoksbergen, 2006, p.336)

Advice: Let your teenager know that you "see" her. Talk about the differences that she experiences and do not stress the similarities. Ask her why she feels like a misfit. Does she feel this way because of how she looks or because her history is different? Does she have the feeling that you do not accept her as she is, or that there is something wrong with her as a person? Try to react as sensitively and responsively as possible, so that your teenager will feel acknowledged. Do not fill in what this means for her. She is

perfectly capable of expressing these sentiments herself. Ask her
how you could help her to feel less of a misfit. Perhaps she has
the need to identify more with other (adopted) children with the
same cultural or ethnic background. Maybe she would like to do
something tangible with her culture. Possibly she really doesn't feel
the need to be busy with her background now. Maybe she only
wants you to accept her for who she is and be more aware of her
qualities.

Try to find out if you are, perhaps unconsciously, disappointed with
your child or with the adoption. If this is the case, you are probably
transferring that disappointment onto your child (see Chapter 6).
If you have birth children in your family, it is important for you to
realise whether or not you really do make distinctions between
them. Perhaps your child intuitively feels that, although you love
her very deeply, you are having trouble with the differences in
temperament and behaviour between her and your birth children.

If only we were a "real" family

As I described above, adopted children experience differences on
various levels. They have a different ethnic background, which
means their heritage is made up of two or even more cultures.
Besides that, adopted children in a mixed family may have a
heightened sensitivity to the differences between them and their
siblings.

Another important reason for feeling different may arise from the
genetic structure that differs from that of the family they are
growing up in. Whenever adopted children say, with a deep sigh,
they wished their family was a "normal" family, most of the times
that does not mean they reject the adoptive parents, but that they
'would rather not experience the pain that accompanies being given
up', and that they would rather 'be genetically connected to this
family'. If they had had a "real" family, there would be no grief over
the adoption and they would be embedded in the genetic structure

of this family. Suzanne (age 12) says to her mother in a television programme:

> I can never be happy again [concerning adoption], because I really don't have anything, no real father, no real mother, no real brothers, no real sisters; in fact, I really have no family. It feels real, but in fact it isn't real, do you understand?
> (From the documentary 'Tussen eten en afwas', IKON 1982)

Twenty-four years later she explains:

> I didn't feel deeply unhappy at that time, but I was really unhappy concerning my adoption; the domain where nothing is real. I saw my adoptive parents as my parents, but really they weren't. The family treated me as a real niece, but because they were more intellectual, I felt insecure and doubted if I really fitted in. They really felt close to each other in a lot of areas that they had in common.
> ('Echt; Suzanne Benne vierentwintig jaar na "Tussen eten en afwas"', *Adoptietijdschrift nr. 4*, 2006)

Advice: Accept the differences. They will be there anyway and it won't help to try to hide them. If you want to help your teenager by pointing out the similarities, she will only experience the differences more strongly. Acknowledge her sadness about this. If she can show her pain, she will be better able to develop, and the chances are greater that she will be able to give the differences a place in her life. Ask your teenager how you can help. She probably sometimes needs to have the differences emphasised. Possibly it will help her if you look for as much information about the adoption as you can find, so she will be able to get to know the facts and start to process them. Perhaps she feels the need to contact other adopted children, or have friends that come from the same ethnic or cultural background. You must also accept that your child will miss a certain primal recognition for the rest of her life.

> I have long been searching for a kind of feeling. The feeling that I'm looking for, that I miss, is hard to put into words. I can only describe it adequately by saying that it transcends the realm of actual "knowledge". Almost like animal knowledge. I'm looking for the feeling that people instinctively understand me, without words. Not because they think they know what I mean, feel or want, but because they recognise my meanings, feelings and wishes within themselves. [...] A part of me is looking for a primal sense of feeling, recognition and understanding. This part of me never really finds ground anywhere, and that results in a rather lonely feeling. [...] From my point of view, a certain part of the "primal recognition" is irreversibly lost between parent and child in adoption.
> (Renée Claassen in Hoksbergen, 2006, p.87)

General advice

- Feelings of rejection, abandonment, shame and guilt are often the result of a negative self-image. Possibly your teenager was less troubled by a negative self-image before but is now experiencing it because of her developing identity and growing consciousness of having been relinquished. Tell your teenager often that she is much valued and loved, and make this clear in several ways, for example, by giving her compliments or individual attention regularly.
- Children do not easily show vulnerable emotions. If your teenager verbally denies these feelings but in her behaviour shows a different attitude towards, for example, a fight with a friend, you could say:

> *You say that you are OK with having a fight with Sofie, but I see that you become quiet when someone mentions her name.*

By naming her contrary behaviour, you are showing your teenager that you are attentive to her emotions as well as her behaviour. Possibly this will make her feel safer, and she will show more of her emotions (see Chapter 7).

- If you have the feeling that your teenager would want to talk about her adoption, but doesn't dare to, you could try saying something like this casually:

  If I were you, I would think a lot about the past. You know absolutely nothing about your birth parents; I would find that frustrating.

  Possibly your teenager will not respond to this. That does not mean she has not heard your remark. Perhaps she needs a little time before getting back to you. Create a safe, open climate in which your teenager will feel safe talking about the adoption. Name her behaviour and her emotions, so she can build up basic trust. Painful emotions can only be felt in an emotionally safe environment.

- Bear in mind that your teenager might be having trouble in school because of her adoption. Giving the adoption a place in her life is something that costs energy and time, and it is quite possible that your teenager doesn't have the concentration necessary for learning. Notify the most important teachers at school about her difficulties with learning at the moment. Try to find a balance between supporting her feelings and stimulating her academic achievements.

- If your teenager is not looking forward to living on her own, it's probably better not to put any pressure on her to leave. That way her fears will probably pass more easily. Try to talk about the moment that she may be leaving the house, make the situation concrete. What will happen? What will she feel, think and do? If she can express her fears, she will be able to understand that they are based on feelings, not on reality. Ask her what it is that she is most afraid of and talk about what you can both do about it. Let her know that she will never be alone, even when she leaves home.

- As a result of the grieving process that your teenager is working through, she may (temporarily) have a younger emotional age than her peers. She may be more vulnerable and more susceptible to risky behaviour and situations. It is important that you keep this in mind and that, if necessary, you pay more attention to her safety than usual. This is also true for other adopted and non-adopted children who have too little basic trust.

- If your teenager is stuck in feelings of fear, sadness and shame, it is important that you show her that her worrying will not get her anywhere. Her feelings may have had a function in the past, but they do not in the present. She is here now, in this world, with this family and with these opportunities. Help her to see that she can also have positive new thoughts, which will probably make her less sad. Help her to identify the moments that make her feel happy, and try to replicate these moments (see Chapter 9). Show her that it's necessary for her to accept responsibility for herself: in the end, she will have to make something of her life.

- If your teenager continues to be stuck in her worrying, do not ask her more questions or make further comments. She may start seeing any form of reaction on your part as a reward. Just give her a confirmation of receipt or name her emotions, express your opinion afterwards and let the subject rest (see Chapter 7).

- If you suspect that your child, due to her disposition or history, has too little basic trust and is fundamentally afraid, sad or uncertain about her adoption, contact an adoption support worker.

6

Pitfalls for parents

Asked about the meaning of life, people start recounting their entire life history.
György Konrád

Introduction

Raising children is a difficult process. As a parent, you will have to find a balance between your own needs and the needs and developmental phases of your child. When you are not functioning well yourself, that has a direct influence on your child's development. Research shows that parents who are not securely bonded often pass on that insecure bonding to their children (Van IJzendoorn, 1994). When someone is unable to bond securely with others, his or her child will most probably not be able to learn how to feel safe with others. A parent's unresolved losses or problematic youth can also have an influence on the child's development; it can lead to the child having problems dealing with emotions like sadness, anger or frustration, or to the parent's having expectations that the child will achieve things that he or she was unable to achieve when young. To be able to function well as a family, it is important that not only your adopted teenager but also you yourself search for the centre of your thoughts and feelings. If not, chances are you will transfer problems from your own youth onto the next generation.

Because your adopted teenager is especially vulnerable and needs even more space than the average child in order to develop properly, it is especially important for him that you know yourself thoroughly and are aware of your own perspective on life. As I wrote in Chapter 2, adopted children often experience a difficult and vulnerable puberty, which means that you, as a parent, must be well prepared. For you, as well as your teenager, puberty can provoke strong confrontations between yourself and your inner patterns and expectations. If, for example, your teenager displays aggressive or rebellious behaviour, you might suddenly hear echoes from the past saying, 'after all, you aren't the "real" father or mother' or 'adopted children are often very problematic'. Perhaps you were warned years ago by friends or relatives that, 'You don't know what you are getting yourself into', and you will suddenly be scared by your teenager's unknown genes, now that he is resisting you so boldly. Perhaps he resembles his birth parents, who may be of a different class and possibly have behaved irresponsibly in the past. Especially in this period full of change, there is a chance that both your teenager's and your own weaker sides will surface and reinforce each other – for example, because you are both afraid of the unknown genes, rejection or loss. You each might also feel that you have to be a superchild or superparent, or you might both feel vulnerable about not sharing a bloodline (see also 'Introduction' in Chapter 2).

In the following pages, I will discuss the thoughts that might influence your behaviour towards and feelings for your child. Even though it is quite possible that some parents will not recognise these thoughts, I want to discuss them here anyway – especially because many parents will, at least in part, be familiar with some of these thoughts and fears. Also, it may be that, even if you are unaware of some of these feelings at first, you may become aware of them later in life. Parents who recognise these thoughts and feelings ("pitfalls") at least to some extent, might be able to understand their inner patterns more easily and, as a consequence, be less influenced by them. If you *dare to look at* your own pain, fear or frustration and eventually are willing to process those feelings, it will be for the good for both your own and your child's development.

My child is suddenly behaving very differently – perhaps he is like his birth parents

Because of hormonal changes, adolescents are often, and quite unexpectedly, confronted with heightened aggressive and sexual feelings. This might frighten you into unconsciously associating this extreme behaviour with your teenager's genetic background. If your child's birth parents were addicted to drugs or alcohol, or if they behaved aggressively, criminally or irresponsibly in any other way, you might be especially likely to fear that your teenager has inherited these traits from them. This feeling will be only stronger if your child has a very different or more extreme temperament that is nothing like yours. If your teenager strongly opposes you and the rules and guidelines you have in the family, you might be tempted to try to strongly control or monitor his behaviour, out of fear that he will adopt the same sexual and socially irresponsible behaviour as his birth parents. Unwillingly, you might be creating a self-fulfilling prophecy. Your child's fear that indeed he has "the genes for bad behaviour" will be confirmed and he will, as a result, start creating even more extreme situations. This might convince him that he is, indeed, a "bad" person and that his adoptive parents would be better off sending him away.

Advice: It is important that you recognise your own fear and start realising that your thoughts and feelings are possibly influencing your child's development in an unconstructive way. Your fear that your child might have inherited "bad" genes is understandable, but is certainly not justified. Yes, children are formed by their genes, but they are formed just as much by the circumstances of their life and youth (see Chapter 1). Do not let your child drown in his own fears. Convince him that he may indeed have some of the same genes as his birth parents, but that his situation is very different and that he can make very different choices than his birth parents did (see 'My parents were bad people, so I am probably bad too' and 'I do not feel at home here' in Chapter 4). Let him know you believe in him and will not abandon him. Acknowledge positive behaviour regularly, and let him know you are really listening to him and hear what he is saying so he will feel acknowledged by you. What your teenager needs is the certainty that you trust him, even though his behaviour might be extreme. When things are calm, try to agree to rules that he should follow. Let him know why you set these rules – for example, to protect him from getting himself into unsafe situations. Show him what might happen if he finds himself in an unsafe situation and what the consequences might be in the long run. Help him to develop responsible behaviour. Do not bind him, but try instead to provide him with freedom, step by step. Reward your child when he succeeds in taking responsibility. If you are not able to break the chain of extreme behaviour, contact an adoption support worker.

We are not his real parents

As an adoptive parent, you have probably been confronted with the fact that 'you are not your child's natural parents' in a number of ways and on a number of occasions (see also 'Identity' in Chapter 2). During your child's puberty, you might be confronted with this fact more than before, especially because the differences between you and your teenager will be more pronounced and, at the same time, your child might feel the need to get to know more about the parents to whom he is genetically connected. You might feel rejected or uncertain because your teenager is not only rejecting you but also seems to love the people who did very little or nothing for him more than he loves you. You might conclude, in silence, that you are probably not a satisfactory father or mother and that your child would indeed have been better off with his "real", birth parents.

Advice: You should realise that the doubts you are having about parenthood can have an influence on your teenager's development. Although he might be confronting you with this problem by saying that 'you aren't his real parents anyway', it is probably not his intention to defeat you completely. It is more likely that, as a result of his adoption, he is trying to achieve exactly the opposite. He wants to hear you say that you will not leave him 'despite all of that', and that you will always be his parent.

You should also realise that your child is an adolescent and as such, will do anything to subvert the rules. This may be the reason why he uses terms like "real parents". However, adolescents need adults to set rules and provide them with guidelines and boundaries. They start feeling unsafe when parents do not fulfil their responsibilities. What a teenager would like to say out loud, but never does, is this:

> **If you love me, you would take care of me and make sure I don't do things that will be harmful.**
> **(Riley, 2005, pp.132–4)**

Precisely for this reason, it is extremely important for your teenager that you do not allow yourself to be defeated, and that you promptly start investigating any doubts you might have about your ability as a parent. If you are afraid of failing or of being rejected, your teenager will intuitively feel this and that can undermine your authority and his self-confidence. His fear that he cannot rely on you and that he is alone (just as he was before) will be confirmed. This may strengthen his anger and his desire to reject you. In discussions, try to maintain a clear separation between the rules and guidelines you have made, on the one hand, and his adoption history on the other. If, for example, he fails to follow the rules and makes it clear to you that he does not feel obliged to do so, precisely because you are not his "real" parents, you might say something like this:

We keep having fights about you coming home too late.
And you keep breaking the rules. Let's first finish this
discussion. Later on, when this argument and your feelings
about this are settled, we'll talk about your feelings about
the adoption.

It is also very important for you to realise that adopted teenagers
have to construct their identity and that birth parents need a place in
that identity. Thoughts like 'My child is not only rejecting me, he
seems to love the people who did little or nothing for him more than
he loves me', are very understandable, but they are not constructive.
It is best for your teenager's development if you accept his birth
parents and give his history and origins a place within your family.

A child of our own would have resembled us more

Parents often have unconscious expectations for their child. For
example, they want him to be happy and they want him to have the
opportunities that they, for whatever reason, did not have. They also
often have unconscious expectations and fantasies that are based
on their idea of the perfect child, the child they dreamed of before
birth. As an adoptive parent, you might be even more vulnerable to
these fantasies, especially if, during puberty, the racial, cultural and
genetic differences between you and your teenager become more
pronounced, or if he starts making unsuitable friends or playing very
loud music. You possibly begin to notice that the birth children of
your friends are calmer, more studious or less combative than your
own. The conflicts between you and your teenager intensify.
Suddenly, you may feel a sense of disappointment and you may ask
yourself what it would have been like to have a child of your own.
Would he have been more like you? Would he have had fewer
troubles at school? Would he have fitted in better with your family?
Possibly you are taken by surprise by these questions and you feel
uneasy because you find that, after all these years, you still have
feelings that are about your unborn baby.

Even if you have adopted for reasons other than because of childlessness through infertility, you may still start dreaming of a genetically similar or a different, nicer child, especially if there is a lack of rapport with you or with the birth siblings in the family. You might be feeling disappointed because your expectations and ideals concerning adoption have not been realised.

Advice: In both cases, the frustration you feel is due to a loss of an ideal. It is important that you discover the roots of your disappointment. If you fail to do so, you are likely to project your imagined child or the ideal that you wanted to achieve onto your adopted teenager, which can be harmful for his further development. Your teenager can probably sense your expectations intuitively and this will confirm his belief that he is letting you down and is, therefore, worthless. Your fantasies can create a snowball effect and make your teenager's feelings of inferiority worse (see Chapters 3, 4 and 5).

It is important that you understand and accept your longing, as well as the fact that your dream is not realistic. All parents have dreams and ideals for their children, especially before they are born. But once they have been born, children develop autonomously and parents have to adjust their dreams and ideals. Expectations are often very high, especially in families with birth children; they often expect their children to be like them and make decisions as they do. The fact that their children eventually do not live up to their expectations is something many parents have to learn to live with. For adoptive parents, the dream of having a birth child has often remained a dream similar to the child's dream about the unknown birth parents. Enduring fantasies are often strong, but they are never realistic.

You can help to boost your teenager's basic trust by connecting with your own inner sadness. Acknowledge your desire, do not feel guilty, talk about your sadness and disappointment to your partner or a good friend; by talking about it, you are giving root to your desires and fears. Try looking at the situation from a more realistic perspective. Accept and embrace the differences. Try to see your teenager for what he is. It is, of course, impossible for him to live up to your imagined ideal or take the place of your unborn child. Make him feel that he is part of your family, no matter what. However ambivalent your adopted teenager's behaviour may be, what he needs most during this period is the safety of a family, the knowledge that he will be accepted even though he is different and that he will not be left. If your teenager feels the need to connect with his ethnicity and culture, try meeting these demands.

I have to make my child happy

Most parents intend to make their child happy. Even though that wish is sincere and is the result of love, it is not always easy for children to deal with that wish. Because of this, children might have the feeling that they 'are only good enough if they are happy and/or successful'. For adoptive families it is even more difficult to deal with this wish, especially because the parents often feel they have to justify why they chose to adopt. Years ago, your child's adoption was a conscious, irrevocable decision that your child had no say in. If your teenager seems unable to find happiness, you may start feeling guilty: 'Why did we feel such a strong need to adopt? Should we have taken him from his natural environment? Were we being selfish or too idealistic?' Perhaps you are trying to prove to yourself that you did indeed take the right decision by adopting your child:

> Our children's happiness, and maybe especially the happiness of our adopted children, is something that means very much to us. Sometimes it feels like an extra responsibility, for it was our ideal in the first place: to provide children who got off to a bad start with a home. Those children deserve a happy ending. Can there ever be enough happiness in the world?
> (from *Adoptietijdschrift nr. 4*, 2006, three-part 'De Adoptieouder')

Trying to justify the reasons for adoption often results in parents trying to do more than their best to make their child happy.

Advice: For a healthy development, adopted children in particular need to feel free to behave in ways that are not socially acceptable and to give expression to feelings of anger, shame, guilt, rejection and abandonment. *Ideally, a child should feel free to feel unhappy.*

This is why you must try to be aware of your own motivation for wanting your child to be happy and why you must make sure that your motivation plays as small a role as possible in the way you raise your child. Your teenager, who is especially sensitive to rejection, can sense your desire intuitively and might not dare to develop autonomously. If he is unable to satisfy your desires, the chances are great that he will start feeling worthless and, in the end, become highly frustrated.

> **I often wonder: Why did you adopt me? You wanted to help a child in need, that's very nice and all, but I didn't ask for it. And now I have to be happy and successful, while I don't even want to be! I wish I had never been adopted, and that I was still in China with my mother.**

It is also important that you realise that parents who gave birth to their children also often have the same feelings of guilt. Asking yourself 'Why did we adopt him?' is in fact the same question as 'Why did we put him on this earth?' The fact that someone was born or adopted into a family does not give the parents the responsibility to make sure the child will become a happy person. Parents can provide the necessary conditions for their child to grow up in. But in the end, it is the child's responsibility to give meaning to his life.

> **We just really wanted kids and so I became pregnant twice. I was really happy that our children turned out to be healthy. I didn't really think much about whether they were going to be happy. They were with us and**

we would provide them with a proper childhood. It was only when our eldest daughter entered puberty that I started having my doubts. When she was fifteen she became depressed and developed an eating disorder. We had trouble getting on, we had lots of fights. She often reproached us for having put her on this earth. In the beginning I could make some sense of this, but after a while it started to sink in. She was so unhappy that I began to feel guilty. Why *did* we put her on this earth? She hadn't asked for it. That much was true. It was really our selfish desire that had caused her to be born. I also felt guilty because she couldn't seem to become happy. For some reason I blamed myself for having given her "the wrong genes", genes that weren't able to make her happy. Putting a child on this earth is an enormous responsibility, but you don't think of that as a young parent. You're creating new life and think you are doing good by doing so. If the child turns out to be unhappy, that's something you can't protect her from. You can only provide the right conditions. In the end they are responsible for their own happiness. That idea really hurts sometimes.

I have to prove to others that it can work out

A lot of adoptive parents have the feeling that they are in a small glass box and that they not only have to prove to themselves, but also to the world, that they can be 'very good parents'. As an adoptive family, you tend to be more in the spotlight and you have to explain yourselves to others more often.

The sounds [of warning] from people in our environment have somewhat diminished [during our kids' upbringing], but I still do have the feeling that people do monitor our adopted children's well-being more closely. Parents in school spontaneously blurt out

their opinions about our adopted children's behaviour and development or the way we deal with them. We did not have the same experience with our [now grown-up] biological children.
(from *Adoptietijdschrift nr. 4*, 2006, three-part 'De Adoptieouder')

Also, negative comments about adoption in the mainstream media can make you feel obliged to defend your family situation to others, or that you have to counter certain prejudices. For this reason alone, you may feel that you need to prove to others that all is well in your family. You may also be experiencing feelings of competition with parents of birth children. If so, you may be unconsciously trying to show that your children can be just as happy and successful as "ordinary" children.

Advice: Feeling that you have to be a better-than-average parent is not a problem in itself. It is true that parents of adopted children need more skills than birth parents (for an overview of these abilities, see Wolfs, 2008, pp.4–5). This must, however, not result in your teenager feeling that he, as a result of your "'good parenthood", has to be a "happy, successful child". The conventional image of a "good parent" is often connected with an impression of how successful and happy the children are. However, for the children themselves, it is more important that a "good parent" provides safety and the possibilities for autonomous development. For your adopted teenager, a super-parent is someone he does not always have to interact with in socially acceptable ways, and who can be told at times that things are not going as well as they should be. Also, to him a super-parent is someone with whom he can have a good cry about trivial things or about his adoption. If it's possible for him to be himself and connect with the pain he feels about his history, he will, in the end, develop a good sense of autonomy. If you are able to support your child in this, whatever the world around you thinks, you are of the greatest importance to him.

I want to spare my child the sadness and pain about his past

One of the hardest parts of raising an adopted child is explaining the adoption story. Due to natural protection mechanisms, you may be inclined to keep painful information from your child, in the hope that he will be spared sadness and anger about what was done to him in the past. You might also be inclined to keep the subject of his adoption out of your child's mind because you feel uncertain about the strong emotions that the truth may trigger in him. Because of this protection mechanism or fear, you might be thinking 'As long as my child does not ask, he doesn't want to know'. This may result in you postponing telling him the truth and in your child only having to find out when he leaves home or sets out to find out about his adoption himself.

Advice: It is wrong to think that painful information is better withheld from children. The truth is that it is better to provide your child with painful information than with no information at all. If he has no information, he may start creating unrealistic fantasies that prevent him from constructing a fitting identity. Besides that, the trust you have built up may disappear when he finds out that you withheld information (see also Chapter 9, 'Creating openness'). It is also a misconception to think that children who do not ask do not want to know. Teenagers in particular, but very young children too, are interested in information about their adoption history. They need this information in order to build their identity. However, they are often also plagued by feelings of shame or fear and therefore they sometimes do not dare to bring up the subject. It is important that you break through this fear of communication and teach yourself as well as your child to talk about this subject. You need to think about whether your protection mechanism, and the fact that you are unwilling to talk, have to do with your own fear of strong emotions. You might not have been able to deal with strong emotions yourself about the past. If so, you would do well to acknowledge this and connect with this pain. If you are able to look back at your own losses with love, not fear, you are more likely to be able to let go of your own strong emotions and stop projecting them onto your teenager.

It is important that you realise that many children, adopted or not, have an intense curiosity concerning their past. Questions like, 'Were you able to feel me in your tummy? Where exactly was I born? In what bed? At what time? Who was there? Did it hurt? Was I healthy?' are important to almost any child.

Try to embrace your child's adoption story and give it a central, distinct place within your family. Painful and complex information must be shared and related during puberty – or better still, beforehand (see Wolfs, 2008).

By creating openness, your teenager will be better able to give shape to his identity. Moreover, he will know that he is supported by his parents in hard times. It may sound paradoxical but you are giving your child a great gift by telling him the truth when he is young. That will help him to give meaning to the facts, especially if these facts are complex and painful.

What is there to talk about? We know nothing of his past

Adopted teenagers usually want to know as much about their adoption story as possible. They want to know more about their birth parents in order to be able to recognise similarities and differences. The reasons why they were adopted are also important; they want to know if they were wanted or not. Often these facts are only partly available, and parents are left to relay what is in the limited adoption files that they received. The result may be that you do not discuss the adoption much, and that your teenager starts fantasising about the details himself. Depending on his temperament, imagination, attachment and history, your teenager will fill in these details positively or negatively. Without you knowing it, he might be creating an idea of his adoption that is completely false and which will block his further development.

Advice: If you are dealing with fear of communication, and if that is what is preventing you from talking about adoption (see above), it is important that you investigate your fear and try to conquer it. When few facts are known, it is especially important to develop a coherent story and to share as much as you know with your teenager. Speculating about what it realistically *might* have been like is better than providing false information or none at all. If you and your child fantasise together, you can create a story that is more realistic, and also give your child a chance to express his fears and reveal his thoughts and emotions about the subject. This will undoubtedly benefit his development.

Become familiar with the political, social and cultural situation of your child's birth country and try to come up with several scenarios concerning the reasons why he may have been given up for adoption. There might be historical, cultural or political documentaries, articles or books available that your child can learn from and identify with. It is also important to be aware of your teenager's ethnic background. He might want to learn things that will connect him to his native country. He might want to adopt certain customs or traditions that are specific to his country. You should find out if he wants to contact other adopted teenagers or young adults with a similar ethnic background. If your child is interested, try to get more information. You may want to contact the orphanage or foster home where your child stayed. You might be able to bring information to light that was previously unknown. However, be sure not to force anything onto your child. He is entitled to developing his own identity at his own pace.

My child longs more for his birth parents than for us

In order to construct a healthy identity, adopted children need information about their birth parents and about the reasons why they were given up for adoption. Because the possibility of an encounter becomes more real every year, they often start fantasising about a possible meeting during this period. Adopted teenagers seem to want to connect to their roots more than ever, while at the same time they are breaking loose from their adoptive family (as every teenager does). The coincidence of these two developments (connecting and breaking loose) may make you feel insecure. 'Does he love us? Would he rather be with his birth parents? He is probably more like them than like us. Soon he will be looking for them and we will lose him.'

Maybe deep inside you are haunted by a fear of communicating and the idea that if your teenager starts talking about his birth parents, his desire for them will only grow stronger. In that case, your fear of rejection and abandonment is keeping you from being open.

Advice: Realise that your teenager may have the same fear of communicating as you do. He may very well prefer not to bring up his birth parents because he fears he will not be loyal to you by doing so. It is likely that in your fear he will see acknowledgement of the idea that he is not allowed to be curious about his birth parents because you will feel rejected if he does. This will probably result in even more fantasising about his birth parents, which will only strengthen his conflict of loyalty. As a result, he will not be able to construct a realistic image of his birth parents and the reason for his adoption. This will prevent him from constructing a fitting identity.

The best thing you can do is to accept the existence of his birth parents and make them a natural topic of conversation. They are just as "real" as you are. Talk about them sometimes, so your teenager will not feel threatened and will know that his birth parents are a safe and natural subject to talk about. If he feels safe, chances are he will automatically start talking about them (at a moment that's right for him).

If you are afraid of rejection and abandonment, it is important for you to investigate this fear. Usually it is the result of one or more experiences of loss or disappointment in the past. If you are able to let in the pain that flows from these life experiences, chances are you will dare to connect more easily with yourself and, as a result, also with your child. In the end, your responses to your teenager will probably be less dependent on these fears.

You must realise that the desire for information in most cases does not mean that adopted teenagers long for a real search for their birth parents, but that they long to know (at least some of) the missing pieces of the puzzle. Most teenagers are looking for a balance between the love they feel for their adoptive parents and their growing curiosity about their birth parents and their adoption.

He will probably be happy to be rid of us

During puberty, many parents become more anxious about rejection, abandonment and loss. Parents of birth children can also experience this very same fear. A teenager's development is centred on the construction of an identity and the process of growing up, which means they will rebel against their parents and start identifying with friends. For adoptive parents, this period is often especially hard to bear, because their teenagers are not only becoming autonomous and leaving home, but also because they will often want to know more about their birth parents and their heritage (see above). Therefore, you may feel you are being rejected twice. In common with many parents of rebellious teenagers, you may possibly feel you are not good enough and as an adoptive parent you may also feel that your teenager's roots are more important to him than you are. Perhaps you are dreading the "moment of truth", the moment your child definitively rejects you because he has not found in you the parent that he seemed to need.

Out of fear of rejection and losing your teenager, you may start setting boundaries for his manifested behaviour by establishing more rules. You might start confronting him more often than necessary or you might start ignoring his behaviour and his desire for more information about the adoption in order to protect yourself from the pain of rejection.

Advice: You should realise that your adopted teenager is just as anxious about rejection and abandonment as you are (see above, and the sections 'It is better if I do not bond too much with people' and 'If I am too rebellious, I will lose my adoptive parents' in Chapter 5); for this reason, there is an increased possibility that he will start misinterpreting your behaviour. He might start to believe that you do not love him and that he is not allowed to be loyal to his birth parents. Your teenager will probably get the feeling that you do not accept him the way he is, which will only exaggerate the differences. To break this downward spiral, it is important for you to investigate your own fears. Your fear might be stronger because of unprocessed grief. You might be feeling that you are not a "real parent" (see 'We are not his real parents' above), which will trigger this fear. Try to deal with earlier experiences of loss and prevent them from exerting too much influence on your role as a parent. Let your teenager know that you love him and that you regret not spending more time with him. You might do something fun together once a week. Let him know that he is a fine person the way he is and that you will never leave him, whatever happens. Even though he is not being sociable, he will probably benefit from a strong, loyal bond in the long run. Let him know that he is absolutely free to long for his birth parents. Ask him what he would like to know about his heritage. You might try to find more information about this, together.

If he leaves home, we will be alone again

As I described above, puberty is a vulnerable period for almost every parent. It is a period in which children create some distance from their parents and start leading their own life to a greater and greater extent. As a teenager gets closer to adulthood, his parents start realising that their role as parents is almost completed and that a farewell to their child is in sight. They are only steps away from a new phase in life and in their relationship with each other. As a result of all these changes, parents are more susceptible to the capricious behaviour of their teenager, who is in fact working through a perfectly healthy process of letting go and is rejecting his parents as part of this process.

Adoptive parents can be especially sensitive to this process of letting go and preparing for the inevitable departure, just as their adopted children can be (see Chapter 5, 'If I leave home, I will be alone again'). For example, the grief about not having been able to conceive can return; your child's tantrums might have caused you to start fantasising about a birth child. There once was a moment when you had to let this dream go, and now you are nearing a similar sort of loss. Your adopted teenager, who, as a child, needed your love and protection so badly, has now started longing for his birth parents. The reality of a possible search may also make you feel anxious; possibly you will lose this child to his "real" parents as well.

As a result of this fear of abandonment, you may be reluctant to provide your child with enough freedom. You may unconsciously start evading the situation by neglecting your child's longings or extreme behaviour, or you may confront him too often. This can lead to your teenager feeling right about his own thoughts and feelings of rejection and abandonment. As a result, he may start becoming even more obstinate or even more introvert and insecure.

Advice: Although your fears have understandable origins, it is nonetheless important that you try to understand and deal with them, so that you will be less inclined to be influenced by them (see above). Adopted children in particular need rock-solid parents who can constrain their emotions and who are not feeling insecure by their teenager's behaviour. In their growth towards independence, teenagers have enough fear and uncertainty on their plates. During this vulnerable phase, they need all the help they can get. You should realise that your child's emotional search for his heritage is a logical result of his development; to be able to shape his identity, your child needs information. Try as early as possible to create a safe and open climate where he can pose his questions and uncertainties about his adoption. The fact that your teenager talks and thinks a lot about his heritage does not mean that he really wants to meet his birth parents. Only some adopted children actually start actively searching, and the ones who do seldom break off all contact with their adoptive parents. In most cases, the ties only strengthen.

Prepare your teenager for the fact that he will be leaving home soon. Talk about the idea of departing and ask him how he feels. Let him know that you will never leave him, whatever happens. That way he will be able to develop the certainty that 'he will not be alone (again)' (see also 'If I leave home, I will be alone again' in Chapter 5).

General advice

- Try to not feel rejected too easily. It is only normal that you are not your child's main focus any more. Teenagers often see their parents as obstacles in the way to independence. When, however, troubles do arise, the child will return to the parents, looking for a safe haven.
- Do not too easily assume that you are not doing a good job. A teenager's brain works differently from an adult's brain. It is important that you help your child to plan and organise, and teach him to be sensitive to other people. Make decisions for him on important issues as long as he is not capable of doing so himself. Make sure that he is safe and do not allow his responses to make you feel insecure. Your teenager wants you to take good care of him. Sometimes he cannot (yet) see what is good for him.
- Make sure you are not influenced by your own fears too much. Fear is often the result of losses from the past that have not been processed. If you find a way to connect to the pain that accompanies these losses, your fear will probably disappear and

you will be free to connect with your child. It is more likely that your teenager will then be increasingly able to be himself and reveal his true feelings. In the end, you can only start trusting others (including your child) when you trust yourself.

- Do not ask too much of yourself as a parent. The more you ask of yourself, the more you will (unconsciously) be asking of your teenager. In the end, no one will benefit. Try to accept yourself as you are. If you love yourself, you will be better able to love and accept your teenager. Consequently, he will dare to connect with you more easily.

- Adoptive parents sometimes try *so* hard that they can hardly react sincerely and from the heart any more. Adopted teenagers in particular have a very strong sense of what is fair and just and what is not. Insincerity can be an obstacle to good contact and can even trigger mistrust. It is better to be really angry sometimes than to always try to do what is right.

- Open yourself to the process of letting go. By the end of puberty, your teenager should be able to take good care of himself. Talk to your child about what kinds of responsibilities he would like to have. Extend these responsibilities gradually if he shows good progress. This will give him self-confidence. Let him know that you will always be his parents and that your relationship will last, even when he is on his own.

- Take good care of yourself. Listening to your own wishes and desires will enhance your feelings of well-being. This will consequently influence the way you deal with stressful situations during this period of your teenager's development. It might have been a long time since you went on a holiday with your partner or took a walk with a friend. If so, this is the time to pick that up again.

- Try to see the positive side of letting go. Maybe it all seems stressful and complicated now, but in the end your teenager will be better able to start his own life. New possibilities for you and your partner will also arise. Think about the future. What is it you would like to do when your teenager leaves home? Talk to your partner about new ways of filling the time and try to enjoy making plans. See if you are harbouring possible fears or uncertainties about your own future. Try to deal with these feelings so that you can move on. Just like your teenager, you will have to be able to make a new start at the end of his puberty.

7

Being sensitive and responsive

In our case, the first ten years were idyllic. Then came puberty. A storm started to rage: lightning flashed, thunder rolled and the roof tiles blew away. What followed for us parents was a period of complete impotence. We saw our sweet girls change, first into little bitches – screaming voices and slamming doors – then into hags that nagged and spat on us, and finally into our archenemies who hated us and did not hesitate to rub that in. War was literally declared. The next five years consisted of us looking on helplessly while they ruined their lives, left school, did everything we forbade them, threw away chances and made choices that would have a long-lasting influence on their lives. We did everything we could to keep communication going.
Jan de Hartog (*Wereldkinderen*, 1991, nr. 3, quote from Juffer, 1999, p.144)

Introduction: the importance of an open, safe environment

Although not all adopted children will experience such a rough puberty as the daughters in the quote above, there will be many families that can at least partially identify with Jan de Hartog's description. In the end, it is a fact that adopted children are more likely to need to put the unconditional parent–child relationship to the test. This makes them more likely to do things that are normally considered wrong like lying, skipping school or stealing. They are, in fact, with their extreme behaviour, putting their parents to the test. In reality, they are asking, 'Well? Do you still love me?' Some children are afraid ever to test this relationship, out of fear of losing their parents for good. Whatever reaction your child displays, the road to independence is, for almost all adopted children, a difficult one. Because, what is left when you lose the people that you do not even share a bloodline with? Femmie Juffer (1999) writes the following:

> The rebellious adolescent dares to openly challenge this [relationship], he defies the laws, while the fearful adolescent would rather not even try. The best thing that adoptive parents can do in these cases, is to keep communicating with their child, or, as Jan de Hartog puts it: do everything you can 'to keep communication going'. In this way, you are providing your child with the coded message: 'We are not giving up. We are not giving you up.' The adopted child, it seems, often asks for this confirmation. (p.146)

By keeping communication going with your rebellious or fearful teenager, you are sending her a message of belonging, saying that she will not be abandoned (again) and also that she is worth the effort and that you respect her thoughts and feelings. That is exactly what adopted teenagers need, even more than "ordinary" teenagers do. They will only dare to show they are angry or sad about their adoption, and long for those "other parents" without shame, if they feel they are in an open and safe environment, where there is no doubt about their relationship with you.

Although it sounds simple, keeping communication going is in fact no easy task, especially with adolescents who do not seem to do anything their parents say and in fact do not seem to want to communicate at all. Parents are often tempted to "just leave their kids alone" – on the one hand, out of a sense of respect towards the child, on the other hand, because they are insecure themselves, often resulting in both parties retreating to their own little islands, widening the gap. Parents in families with teenagers who do hardly any talking usually increasingly become "lecturers", while, in fact, the relationship should become more equal. Keeping quiet hardens differences, forcing parents into drawing sharper boundaries and setting stricter rules, while their child gets more and more angry and rebellious. Everyone retreats into the trenches, so to speak. Starting a sincere and open conversation is often now no easy task, especially because there is no shared sense of trust.

Maintaining mutual trust and respect is, in fact, the most important prerequisite for a good, two-way conversation. Only when your teenager feels that this respect exists, will she feel safe and dare to share her thoughts with you. Her doubts and uncertainties concerning adoption and your unconditional relationship will only become subjects of conversation if she knows that she is fine as she is and that you accept her with all of her thoughts, feelings and desires. Only on this basis is it possible to try, as Jan de Hartog did during this hectic period, to 'keep communication going'.

You can create an open and safe environment by approaching your teenager in a sensitive and responsive way: by carefully listening and observing her (therefore being "sensitive") and by reacting adequately (therefore being "responsive"), she will start to feel "noticed" and understood (Polderman, 1998, pp.422–33). This two-way process will help her to develop a sense of self – she develops a feeling of having a right of existence, an "I-awareness". As a result, she will probably dare to be more herself. During the 1990s, adoption specialist Nelleke Polderman discovered the great effectiveness of reacting sensitively and responsively with adopted children and developed a method of communication in which giving *confirmation of receipt and naming/identifying behaviour and emotions are central*. In this chapter I will describe her principles of interaction, which were derived from *Video Home Training* by Harry Biemans. Adoption support workers (but also social workers who deal with genetically connected families) use similar interaction principles. By giving a confirmation of receipt and naming/identifying behaviour and emotions, parents and children often learn to communicate with each other (again). (I dealt with this subject in *Adoption Conversations: What, when and how to tell*, 2008. In that book I aimed my research at children aged up to 12, but in this sequel, I am focusing on teenagers.)

Biemans and Polderman's interaction principles (see appendix and Polderman, 2004, 2006) (together with the establishment of safe boundaries) are the most elementary means of providing your teenager with basic trust and keeping communication going. In fact, it means you are giving subtitles to what your child does, feels, thinks and wishes. You are making clear (at first without giving your own opinion), verbally or non-verbally, that you have noticed your teenager's initiative. Moreover, you are repeating (in slightly different words) what your child is saying. Your teenager feels that you have seen and heard her. By doing so, you are functioning as a mirror for your teenager, and, as a result, she will gain more self-respect. Being actively seen and heard is very important for teenagers; although their behaviour often doesn't seem to point in that direction, teenagers are continuously looking for acknowledgment and respect. This is even more true for adopted teenagers. Cris da Silva writes about his late teens:

> I always wanted to be the centre of attention.
> Everything had to be about me, at work as well as at home. I tried to get that attention in negative ways: by lying, bursting out in rage or taking things. It took me a while to find that out, for that to sink in. I was about 18 years old, I think. I did notice that people in trouble often came to me for help or advice. I was always there, even when they dumped me afterwards. That

> **attention from others gave me a sense of being, a feeling I really needed.**
> (in Hoksbergen, 2006, p.155)

Polderman's interaction principles are based on a couple of steps in communication (see Appendix 2). In response to an initiative or reaction from your teenager, you may want to take these three steps:

Step 1: Receiving the action or child's initiative (by naming/identifying or giving a confirmation of receipt).

Step 2: Giving your own opinion, feeling, thought or wish.

Step 3: Asking for the opinion of the child concerning what you just said.

It is very important, especially with teenagers, not to forget the third step. By applying Step 3, you are giving your teenager the opportunity to show what she thinks. Now you can confirm what she said again (Step 1), etc. In this way she will feel that she is being treated as an equal, and that her opinion counts for something. To get a better grip on the several steps, I elaborate on them in this chapter. (I have based my research largely on Nelleke Polderman, 2004.)

Step 1: Actively receiving your teenager's initiative

One way to improve the relationship between yourself and your teenager is to actively receive what she says, does, feels, wishes or thinks. This is the first step in the progressive scheme. To establish a natural sequence in the process of communication, it is important to take the second step, in which you give your own opinions. Step 2 will be discussed fully in the following section, but I will include this step (giving your own opinion) in the following examples, because without Step 2 the conversations would sound unnatural. For now, however, I will discuss the theory behind Step 1 only.

By actively receiving your child's initiative (Step 1) your child will realise that she is being listened to and seen: her words are being "heard" and her behaviour and emotions are being "seen". This will have a positive influence on internal communication. You can receive your child's initiative in two different ways:

- without words: you are receiving her words or behaviour by displaying interested body language or intoning positively;
- with words: you provide a confirmation by repeating (preferably in different words) or summarising what your child is saying, or by naming her behaviour, feeling, wish or thought.

Receiving without words

During infancy, when a child is unable to communicate with words, almost all parents naturally use many expressive, non-verbal means by which they try to acknowledge what a child is saying with her baby talk. It is, however, very important that in the years thereafter, you keep on showing that you hear what your child has to say with non-verbal means. This can be done by nodding, making eye contact, intoning in a friendly way, etc. Examples of non-verbal communication are:

- the warmth of your voice;
- facing your child;
- the use of gestures;
- the making of eye contact;
- the friendliness of your expression;
- the way in which you nod or say 'yes' or 'oh'.

If your non-verbal attitude during a short or longer conversation is active, attentive and open, your teenager will (unconsciously) recognise your interest. This interest will make her feel acknowledged. Now she will feel safer and develop more self-awareness.

Receiving with words: providing a confirmation of receipt

If your teenager is giving her opinion or trying to tell you something, you can receive those words by repeating them in a slightly different way or by summarising them. If you were to do this literally, it would sound mocking for a teenager. Providing your child with verbal confirmation is like holding up a neutral mirror; it shows her she has been heard:

> *Teenager: School was really bad again today. There was this new teacher for mathematics. He didn't have a clue where we were, so we had to explain that a hundred times. And then he gave us this really hard problem to solve, too. As if I'm not busy enough already. This way it's really hard to keep up a schedule.*
>
> *Parent: You had a bad day, it seems. Another new mathematics teacher and a new problem to solve. You had your homework all planned and now you have to start all over.*

Repeating what your teenager says *literally* has a boomerang effect, especially because it sounds mocking to them. If, however, you can repeat or summarise her words just a little differently in Step 1, she will feel heard and taken seriously. She will start talking more easily to you now. Moreover, she will be open to your position or opinion. Giving a confirmation of receipt can also provide a point of rest in the conversation, for example, when your teenager is very angry or frustrated:

> *Teenager: I have to do everything in this household. Why do Chiara or Chun never help?*
>
> *Parent: You feel that you are the only one who has to do things in this household. You would like it if Chiara or Chun would help sometimes.*

By putting forward your child's words in this way and not in a question, you are able to lull your teenager's angry mood and bring some peace to the conversation. Asking a question will raise the tone of your voice at the end of the sentence. This automatically leads to the necessity to answer. This is not the case by putting forward a neutrally formulated sentence. The tone of your voice will drop at the end of the sentence. A question – 'You think you have to do everything in this household?' – might also give your teenager the idea that you are questioning her, so she will want to react defensively to that automatically.

Giving a confirmation of receipt is especially effective when you want to keep the conversation going. It is at the same time, a way of probing more deeply. I will discuss this in the next chapter.

Receiving with words: naming/identifying behaviour, feelings, wishes and thoughts

Instead of repeating your teenager's words with different ones, or simply summarising them, you may also choose to name the behaviour, feelings, wishes or thoughts behind the message (for example: 'You must be really tired', or 'You sound sad'). Your teenager will then have the feeling that not only is she being heard verbally, she is also being seen emotionally: you are showing that you perceive her inner world. This method will prove to be especially useful for teenagers who lack basic trust. If you name behaviour, feelings, wishes and thoughts, they will learn to experience themselves (who am I, what am I feeling, etc) and they will learn that they have a right to be there, that they are fine as they are. This can be especially helpful for teenagers in developing an identity and making it possible for them to be themselves more readily in a group.

Just as when you are giving a confirmation of receipt, it is important that when naming behaviour and emotions, you react neutrally, so that your own opinions do not intrude. Only in this way will your teenager feel truly seen. As soon as she senses the presence of your own opinion, she will experience your reaction as less open and less objective. In a sentence like, 'You are being irritating' or 'You're late again', your own opinion resonates in the background; it would be better to say, 'You're teasing your brother all the time and he really doesn't like that', or 'You are home late again and you promised that you would be on time'. Your opinion or feelings are reserved for Step 2 (see the next section).

Naming behaviour and emotions is subject to five criteria. It must:

- be affirmative (not questioning);
- be neutral (objective, free of your own opinion);
- be concrete;
- begin with 'you';
- refer to the here and now.

It is important that you provide subtitles for your child's action or initiative in the here and now:

- You say what she is doing ('You're throwing your bag in the corner' or 'You're looking at my boots').
- You say what she is feeling ('You are feeling sad' or 'You really hate it that we don't agree').
- You say what she wants ('You want to go to school without a jacket' or 'You would like to go on using Messenger/Facebook').
- You say what she is thinking ('You are thinking…' or 'You are doubting whether you feel like it').

If your teenager is angry and you want to name that, it is important not to say 'You are angry', because this often only increases anger. It is better to name the reason for the anger: 'You are really upset because you cannot go out with your friends tonight.'

You can learn naming behaviour and emotions step by step. Try, for example, to start by only naming the behaviour, feelings, thoughts or wishes in an affirmative, neutral way and then try to give your own opinion (this is Step 2, the sentences in brackets, which I explain in the next paragraph):

- 'You are out of school early today' or 'You are home early.' ('Something must have happened in school.')
- 'You are eating all the crisps.' ('You must be hungry.')
- 'You would probably like a cup of tea.' ('You're sitting there reading, so cosy.')
- 'You look tired' or 'You must be tired after that difficult exam yesterday.'
- 'You are probably sad because you miss Jochem.' ('Jochem was a very sweet cat.')
- 'You probably imagined that I had not thought of that.' ('I tend to forget these things, but this time I didn't.')
- 'You almost never use Messenger or Facebook any more.' ('I noticed that you're hanging around a lot less often with your girlfriends lately.')
- 'You're so quiet.' ('You don't seem very happy. It happens often when you get out of school.')
- 'You're so helpful today.' ('You probably want to ask if you can come home a little later tonight.')
- 'You skipped school.' ('You probably have a reason for that.')
- 'You are beaming. ('You probably had a good time in school.')
- 'You're so quiet.' ('You are probably still thinking about the conversation we just had.')

If you have suspicions about why your child is acting in a certain way, you may want to express those suspicions by naming them:

- Possibly you are sad because you feel different from the other kids in class.
- Maybe you hit that boy because he is always teasing you.
- You are probably so angry because we know nothing about your birth parents.

You might be scared to express such suspicions about your teenager's feelings or thoughts because you may be filling in her feelings for her. Chances are, however, that putting forward these suspicions (neutrally) will have a positive effect on further interaction. If you are correct, she will feel seen and understood by your statement. She will probably elaborate on your suspicion and show her emotions. If she is feeling angry for some other reason, she will surely tell you. She will deny your suspicion and probably tell you what is wrong. What is especially important is that she sees that you are trying to understand her.

If you are uncertain about what your teenager might be feeling, you may want to limit yourself to naming or identifying her behaviour (Step 1). Now you are free to give your opinion about that (Step 2):

- You've been on that couch all day. Maybe you are feeling sick.
- You keep staring at the floor. I would really like to know what just happened in school, but maybe you would rather not talk about it.

Step 2: Reacting to the initiative

After actively receiving your teenager's initiative, a second step has to follow (unless your teenager reacts immediately after Step 1). This second step has to be a personal reaction to what you have summarised or repeated in Step 1. You might, for example:

- give your own opinion;
- make yourself explicit (feelings, thoughts);
- deepen the conversation by probing more deeply;
- give a compliment;
- make a suggestion;
- name oppositions;
- prompt positively;
- involve other people around.

By means of this second step you are often telling your teenager something about your own feelings and ideas. This is important for her development, because she will learn to:

- develop empathy;
- construct her identity more effectively, because she knows what you think of her;
- nurture a feeling of safety because you are reliable in your opinions;
- take into consideration other people's opinions;
- form her own opinions.

The second step will also make the first step sound more natural, less formal. It is also a good way to take the lead as a parent:

- You'll be celebrating your birthday in a couple of weeks. I wonder what you will want as a present from us. (make yourself explicit)
- You've finished your homework. That was fast. (give your own opinion)
- You're feeling bad because you cannot join your friends. I can well understand that you want to go with them, but Sunday is your grandparents' wedding anniversary and I would really like you to come. (make yourself explicit)
- You are all shook up by that bad grade. I understand. It's no fun when you're the only one with such a low grade. Maybe Maria can help you with chemistry next time. (make a suggestion)
- You made up with Janine. I really appreciate that. (make yourself explicit and give a compliment)
- So you don't want to go to dancing lessons with Brit anymore because she gossips about you. I wonder why she started doing that suddenly. What do you think, Maria? You know Brit too. Do you have any idea why she started gossiping about your sister? (make yourself explicit and involve other people around)

If your teenager is doing something that you do not approve of, it is best to positively prompt her after giving a confirmation of receipt. This means that you say what you would like her to do, not what you wouldn't.

- So you'd rather not go to camp this summer. I understand. You would rather join your friends on a holiday. I think it is a little early for that. When you're 18, I will allow it.

- You want to go upstairs to chat with your friends online. That is really fun of course. Your friends are probably all online now. I would rather have you stay at the table until everyone is finished, though.
- You don't want to tidy up your room. I'm fine with the fact that you want to have it the way you like it and I won't force you to clean it every day, but I would like you to clean it up once a week so that I can use the vacuum cleaner in there.'
- You are irritated because you always have to be home by one o'clock. But most of your friends have to be home by then, too. When Mickey turns 16, I'll talk to his parents about it. Perhaps you could come home half an hour or an hour later together.

By stressing the things that *are* possible, you are positively directing your child's unacceptable behaviour. This will set boundaries and provide clarity. Besides reacting sensitively and responsively, giving clarity and (certain) boundaries will provide your teenager with the safety that she needs to develop well.

By first using Step 1 (giving a confirmation of receipt or naming behaviour, wishes, thoughts or feelings) and then prompting positively, your teenager will feel seen and heard. She will be less easily obstructed by her own emotions and will be more open to your words, so that conflict situations can sometimes be prevented.

Step 3: Asking for confirmation of receipt or for an opinion

Asking for a confirmation of receipt after giving your own opinion (Step 2) is especially important with teenagers. It is important that they can give their own opinion or reaction, because in this way they will feel that they are your equal. They get the respect that they want so badly. If you ask your teenager how she felt about your words, you are implicitly saying you are taking her seriously and that you value her opinion. Examples of questions are:

- What is your opinion about what I just said?
- I am curious about how that feels to you.
- Would you care to respond to that?
- What is your opinion about that?
- How does this strike you?
- What would you do?

Make sure that you are not filling in answers to your questions. For example, by asking questions like, 'Are you alright with that?' 'Are you hurt by that?' or 'Are you happy/sad about that?' 'Does that make you feel relieved?', you are restricting the answers your child can give. That is because in these questions there are subjective notions that express a feeling (good, hurt, happy, sad, relieved). You are filling in feelings that your teenager may or may not have about what you said in Step 2, and so you are directing your child in her answer. If you use neutral, objective words, there are far more ways for her to express her opinion. The most honest and objective answers follow from open, objective questions:

- What do you think about that?
- How do you feel when I say that?
- What does it feel like for you?
- What do you think about this plan?

If your teenager has difficulty expressing her own opinion or feelings, you might, however, help her by using subjective words. You could, for example, give her a choice between two emotions. She can then think about which of the two best fits her feelings and accept or reject your suggestion.

- I take it you are not happy with this. Am I wrong?
- Do you feel unfairly treated by what I've said, or is it OK?
- You probably agree. Or am I wrong?
- Surely you understand that I'll get worried. Or do you think that's nonsense?

You may want to repeat in different words what was said:

> *Teenager: I'm not going along to Aunt Tessa's, tomorrow. I've got way too much to do.*
>
> *Parent: So you want to stay home. (Step 1, confirmation of receipt) I would really appreciate it if you went along. Aunt Tessa is turning 50 and she is really fond of you. She is looking forward to you coming, just like your cousins. (Step 2, giving your own opinion) How do you feel about that? (Step 3, asking confirmation of receipt)*

Your teenager can now say how she feels about her aunt and can also let you know what she thinks she still has to do. As a parent, you can react to that by giving another confirmation of receipt and by giving your opinion. Now you can ask for another confirmation of receipt in response to that.

> *Teenager: Of course I feel bad for Aunt Tessa. But I have so much homework, I don't know when to do it all.*
>
> *Parent: You don't want to go because you have so much homework. (Step 1). I see that it's hard for you to plan your weekly tasks – it is a lot actually for this week. Maybe I can help you with something so that you'll be free tomorrow anyway. (Step 2 giving your opinion and prompting positively) What do you think about that idea? (Step 3)*

Other examples of conversations in which the parent takes three steps:

> *Teenager: I want to stay out until half past one tonight. Quinton can, too.*
>
> *Parent: You want to be home half an hour later. I am surprised to hear that Quinton can come home at half past one. His parents are always fairly strict. Aren't you a little surprised?*

> *Teenager: Mmm... (silence) Actually, I'm not sure. He was going to ask his parents this afternoon but he said he was pretty sure.*
>
> *Parent: So Quinton also has to ask his parents. Then I suggest that I call his parents and discuss it with them. What do you think?*

or (a different ending to the same example):

> *Teenager: I was also surprised, but Quinton is really allowed to.*
>
> *Parent: So Quinton can come home that late. I am surprised. If he is really allowed to come home that late, I will allow it too. I do want to call his parents and talk this over, because I want you to be home safe tonight. What do you think about that?*
>
> *Teenager: If you want to call that's up to you. But it is not necessary, we will be home safe.*
>
> *Parent: You feel safe and do not think it is necessary to call. I trust you two. But I would like to speak to Quinton's parents anyway.*

Another example in three steps:

> *Teenager: I want to do that paper round because I need the money.*
>
> *Parent: You want to do the early paper round because you are saving up for a new bicycle. I think it is fine that you want to earn money this way, but I want you to get enough sleep, so you will have to be in bed early. What do you think about that?*

Teenager: I can handle an hour less sleep.

Parent: You think you can function with less sleep. But your concentration in school will drop and I will not agree to that. Again, I am fine with you earning money with a paper round but it is hard work getting up so early every morning. I can only allow it if you go to bed on time. What do you think?

Teenager: Well, if you insist I will. Can I call the paper now to say that I can start next week?

Parent: You are willing to agree to my conditions and get going right away. Nice to see you so enthusiastic. Shall we sit around the table tonight and discuss what time you'll be going to bed?

Conclusion

In this chapter I have discussed a method of communication and interaction that will result in your teenager feeling safe and noticed. The method allows her to build up more basic trust and, as a result, she will possibly dare to show more of herself in conversations. Also, you will be able to keep communication going more easily.

In the next chapter, I elaborate on techniques for asking questions that you may want to use along with the three steps discussed in this chapter. Especially when you are having a complex conversation with your teenager, it can be helpful to know what effect certain questions might have on her.

8

Following-up

What it comes down to is to activate the brain to "on".
Teenagers love to use their brain. This way you will be able to
connect with them on a deep level, and really make contact with
them.
Martine Delfos (2005a)

Introduction: summoning up your teenager's own expertise

During a longer conversation, you could easily alternate between
asking for a confirmation of receipt and asking follow-up questions.
This may be necessary, for example, because you might otherwise
have misunderstood your teenager's words or because you want
him to be more specific about his feelings. In that case, you are
asking additional questions about exactly what your teenager said.
In fact, such a question can be seen as a variation on Step 3 in
Polderman's interaction-model (see Chapter 7): you are not asking
for an opinion, but are asking a follow-up question, for example:

Teenager: I want to babysit at Anna and David's so I can make some money.

Parent: You want to babysit for them because you could use some money. I thought you still had quite a bit of savings left. Do you have a plan for this money?

Sometimes giving a confirmation of receipt (Step 1) can be enough to make your teenager want to continue talking. You are asking a question in the most neutral way possible, by repeating the spoken words or summarising them, or you are naming/identifying your teenager's feelings:

Teenager: I don't feel well. I really had a bad day. So many things happened.

Parent: You do look shook up. Sit down, I'll make you a cup of tea. So, you had a bad day?

Asking follow-up questions, together with actively receiving your teenager's initiative, is the most important means of communication that you have at your command. Teenagers want to be raised democratically. In other words, they want to be heard and respected and they stick their fingers in their ears when you start to lecture them. This is even more true for adopted teenagers. By listening, asking questions and exchanging opinions, you are letting your teenager decide and think for himself, and usually there is a lot more space for new answers. This method of questioning is often referred to as "the Socratic method". The Socratic method (based upon the thoughts of the famous Greek philosopher Socrates) takes for granted that man is capable of thinking for himself and that the other can bring out this expertise by directing this thinking process. The best way to do so is by asking questions, instead of telling or filling in. In this way, every human being can discover who he or she really is. Parents can well apply this wisdom to their teenager (who is growing to adulthood). By reacting sensitively and responsively, and asking the right questions, you will be able to bring out your child's own expertise and abilities. Even if the conversation is a painful one, he can still walk away with a good feeling about himself because, through your sensitive position and your interested questions, he will find out how his feelings are structured or where his feelings come from.

Older teenagers in particular (those aged 16 to 18) flourish verbally using this method. According to Delfos, children in this phase are 'verbal canons' and this is the period of the (sometimes a bit naïvely formulated) 'grand ideas' (Delfos, 2005a, pp.216–7). But younger teenagers can, as a result of this questioning method, also begin to develop a sense of equality and independence. They will, however, need more conversational frameworks because they will probably not be able to fully work through a logical problem yet.

By having a Socratic dialogue with you, your teenager will also get a chance to identify to some extent with adulthood. By not preaching or judging, but providing your child with the possibility to answer and think for himself, you are making it possible for him to direct an important part of his own life. You are also making your role as a parent less dominant, something that is important for your changing role. It is, however, important to realise that asking follow-up questions is more effective for teenagers who have sufficient basic trust. Teenagers who lack sufficient basic trust may feel obliged to answer. If that is so, you may want to consider "naming" (in a neutral, objective manner), see Nelleke Polderman's method (see also 'General advice' below).

If you want to ask follow-up questions about what your child is saying or doing, it is important to know which types of questions can lead to particular types of answers. Neutral questions and remarks will probably give your child a lot of space to decide how he will react, while direct questions may give rise to objections. However, in certain situations direct questions can be very effective. In the following paragraphs, I discuss the different sorts of questions and show in what way your questioning method can influence the conversation. (I addressed these questions to some extent in *Adoption Conversations: What, when and how to tell*, 2008, but my focus here is on the experiences of teenagers.)

Direct questions

Direct questions end with a question mark. They have a
questioning tone. In asking direct questions you run the risk of
giving your child the feeling that he is obliged to answer. This
may have an influence on the spontaneity and truthfulness of
the answer. It is, however, not the case that a direct question will
always have such an effect; that would mean you could never ask
your child a direct question.

How your child reacts is dependent partly on his temperament.
A child who is inclined to talk easily and frequently will be less
likely to feel attacked by questions than a more introverted child
will. Sometimes it will depend on the teenager's mood. Especially
during puberty, your child may have periods of heightened
sensitivity and at those times he may feel more threatened by direct
questioning.

There are two ways to handle a direct question. One way is
characterised as *open* questioning, and the other as *closed*
questioning. You can alternate between both types of questions
during a conversation, depending on what it is you are hoping to
achieve.

Open questions

Open questions are those that give your teenager enough space to
answer according to his own insight. He decides how much he tells
you and how long his answer takes. This kind of question is handy
when you want to gain insight into a certain emotion, thought or
fantasy. Open questions often start with 'How' or 'What do you
mean by':

- How did that feel?
- What do you mean?
- What do you think your birth mother looks like?
- What can we do about this?
- What do you mean? Tell me.
- How did you do that?

Open questions can be effective if you do not know what your child's feelings or thoughts about a certain subject are. Older teenagers (16 to 19) especially are capable of answering these kinds of questions clearly. Using an open question, you are inviting your teenager to give a broad account, by which you will both gain better insight into his state of mind. Afterwards, you will be able to ask follow-up questions about specific aspects:

- What do you mean by "not being allowed to be sad"?
- You say that you don't want to see your father because he is nasty to you. Can you tell me what it is that he does?
- So you have made up. How do you feel about that?

If you want to discuss a delicate topic with your teenager, you may also choose to start with a general, open question. This question will indirectly touch upon your child's situation. If you suspect that your child is being bullied in school, but is reluctant to tell you about it, you may start with open, general questions like:

- What do you think about bullying?
- Who are the bullies in your school?
- Which kids in your class are being bullied?
- How do you feel if someone you know well is being bullied?
- What do you do about it?
- Do people sometimes bully you?

You might not want to use "why" questions. Your teenager will feel as if he has to justify his words.

'Why aren't you doing well in school? Why don't you work harder?' Those questions drove me crazy. I felt attacked, got the feeling that I did everything wrong. I found it even harder to tell what was really going on. I usually gave vague answers, like: I didn't feel like school or I didn't do my homework. Sometimes I would just walk away.

(Quote from Dutch parenting magazine *JIM pubers nr. 4*, April 2007, 'Zonder mandaat begin je niks')

"Why" questions often backfire because your teenager feels as if he has to defend himself. That is because there is always an implicit accusation in them. A question like: 'Why did you fail that test?' is better replaced by a "how" question: 'How will you be able to get a good grade next time?'

"How" questions, as opposed to "why" questions, always deal with solutions. This is a much more effective method for communicating with a teenager. You are shifting your focus from negative behaviour towards positive behaviour in the future. Your child will gain insight into his own behaviour and you are also teaching him to look for solutions himself.

Closed questions

These are questions that your child will be able to answer with only one or two words (probably only 'yes' or 'no'). These questions usually block further communication. They will not get your child talking. Nonetheless, closed questions can be very effective for opening a conversation or giving it a certain twist. You can use closed questions when open questions are "too broad" to handle a delicate subject, or if your child is not a great talker. A conversation might open with one or more closed questions. Then you can ask an open question:

- Are you enjoying the new subjects in school?
  What do you like best?
- Are there also things you don't like?
  What do you dislike about them?

Or:

- Do you ever think about your birth mother?
  Are you ever sad when you think about her?
  Do you ever fantasise about her? That she is really friendly or very unfriendly?
  I wonder, how (un)friendly do you think your mother is? What is her life like? Does she have any other children? What do you think?

By asking closed questions, you are providing the conversation with a certain structure, which can be very helpful, especially if your teenager is "drowning" in his emotions and if, as a consequence, he does not know where to start or what to say.

If you have the feeling that he wants to say something but doesn't know how because his thoughts about it are unclear, you might want to ask "closed multiple-choice questions":

- Shall we go out to dinner on your birthday or would you rather do something else?
- Are you frustrated because you can't stop thinking about that bad grade, or is there something else going on?
- How did it go with Jason today? Did you make up or did you not get around to that yet?
- What do you think about this solution? Are you happy, or would you rather think about another solution altogether?

By providing your teenager with clear-cut choices, you will probably help him to get in touch with his true feelings: I don't want this, I want that, that's not what I'm feeling, this is what I am feeling. Your child is handed a structure to work with, which feels safe. He will be able to find out whether what you're saying is true and, in this way, find out what he is feeling and what he wants. You are providing autonomy and the belief that his wishes and feelings matter.

Neutral, affirmative sentences

Neutral sentences can function as follow-up questions. They do not end with a question mark, but with a simple full stop. Because of the neutral intonation, they are less threatening than direct questions. Your teenager will not feel the obligation to answer. He will be less likely to shut off and less inclined to give the socially acceptable answers.

If your child is not a talker, or if he is going through an emotionally sensitive period, you might want to put most questions to him in this way. In fact, this is the same as actively receiving what your child is saying or doing (Step 1, Chapter 7).

By not ending sentences with a question mark but with a full stop, you are creating a quiet, neutral atmosphere and are not letting yourself get drawn into your child's emotions. Your child will also not have the feeling that he is obliged to answer. He has a free choice. This way he will feel more respected and will be more inclined to react.

Neutral, affirmative sentences can be formulated in three ways:

- naming/identifying non-verbal behaviour or emotions;
- repeating the spoken words or summarising them;
- neutrally guessing about your child's feelings.

Naming non-verbal behaviour or emotions

Young people do not show their feelings very easily. They do not possess the necessary vocabulary or cannot find the right nuance. They are, nonetheless, showing enough of themselves through their behaviour and emotions that can easily tell you about which things you need to talk. It is crucial that you learn to recognise these non-verbal signals, for example: he is shrugging his shoulders, staring at the ground, twitching his fingers, nervously biting his hair or nails, not looking at you while you are talking, sitting in his room all day, looking away whenever the word "adoption" is mentioned, starting to do other things to avoid the conversation, or saying that "nothing is wrong", while he is showing with his behaviour, defensive position and intonation that the opposite is true. Bad grades, stomach aches and eczema-like rashes can also be non-verbal signs that your teenager is not functioning well.

Naming or identifying non-verbal behaviour and emotions in a neutral way is a sensitive-questioning technique:

> *You're staring at the ground.*
> *(indirectly you are asking: Are you feeling uncomfortable?)*
>
> *You're shrugging your shoulders.*
> *(indirectly asking: Are you not interested?)*
>
> *You look rather sombre.*
> *(implicitly asking: What is wrong with you? Why are you so quiet?)*
>
> *You don't seem to be feeling well.*
> *(implicitly asking: Why do you keep reacting so angrily lately?)*

It is very likely that your teenager will react to the naming of non-verbal behaviour or emotions; usually it is not necessary to explicitly ask the direct questions in parentheses.

Sometimes teenagers say one thing, but act in a contradictory way. Usually the behaviour or intonation says more than the words themselves. You can effectively ask follow-up questions about this by naming the contradiction in the message.

Parent: You say that it doesn't matter to you, but you keep running upstairs whenever we mention the adoption.

Teenager: I feel bad talking about it.

Parent: You feel bad because it hurts you.

Teenager: No, that's OK.

Parent: So that's not why you run upstairs. So why do you?

(Teenager shrugs shoulders.)

Parent: You're shrugging your shoulders. (Do you not want to talk about it?)

Teenager: I don't know.

Parent: You can't explain.

Teenager: I'm so different.

Parent: You do look different than we do. And because you feel bad about that, you don't want to talk about it.

(Teenager grabs the remote control and puts on the television.)

Parent: You'd rather watch telly. You don't have to talk about it if you don't want to. I can well understand that it might be hard for you to talk about the differences. But you can't close your eyes to them. If you ever want to talk about them, you know we are here. You are a part of this family and if it is up to us, you always will be.

This is a good place to stop the conversation. You have made it clear that you noticed his emotion and that you have seen the shrugging. Your teenager has kept his dignity, because you respect his wish not to talk now and you have also given an opening for him to respond to in the future.

Sentences like 'You look so sombre', 'You're so quiet', or 'You collapsed with a deep sigh onto the sofa. You probably had a bad day' often function as follow-up questions. They will make your child feel that you have seen him and he will probably want to share his emotions with you, at least partially.

If your teenager is not very talkative and you suspect he is unable to express his emotions adequately, you may want to speculate about his feelings in a neutral, affirmative way. It is very likely he will recognise the feelings, especially because you know your teenager well. He will validate his feelings and possibly also try to explain them. If you have interpreted his emotions incorrectly, he will tell you this also. Your teenager will probably now elaborate on the feeling he does have:

> *You are probably sad because you don't know anything about your biological parents.*

> *You feel left out because you look different.*

> *You feel bad because you feel like you were our second choice.*

If you recognise anger in your child, it is important that you do not only name the emotion but also the (probable) reason, because only naming the anger might generate more anger.

Repeating or summarising the teenager's words

When you repeat or summarise what your teenager has said in slightly different words (thus giving a confirmation of receipt), you are also implicitly following up in a neutral way. You are giving a confirmation of receipt without Step 2. If, through your summary, your teenager becomes more aware of what he said, he will probably talk more about it (or explain what he meant in different words). Neutrally repeating or summarising can function like follow-up questions. It stimulates the other person to continue. For example, your child might say:

I am happy that Roel is my brother.

You might answer with a confirmation of receipt:

You like having Roel as a brother.

Often a teenager will continue only because of this last sentence (which, in fact, is only repeating what he said earlier):

Yes, because Roel is also from Brazil.

Now you can interpret your child's words in an affirmative way, possibly also asking if your interpretation is right:

> **Parent: You mean that you like it that you are not the only one in the family who looks like he is from Brazil. Am I right?**
>
> *Teenager: He just went through the same thing.*
>
> **Parent: And that makes you feel less lonely.**
>
> *Teenager: Yeah. Sometimes I just think it's stupid.*

You now might want to consider following up on the subjective word 'stupid' (see also 'Following up in reaction to subjective words' below):

What do you think is stupid then?

You may also want to alternate between giving a neutral

confirmation of receipt and giving your own opinion or asking a direct question (a second step):

> *Parent: You've been eating so little, lately.*
>
> *Teenager: Yeah.*

> *Parent: Aren't you hungry?*
>
> *Teenager: No.*

> *Parent: You aren't hungry. But having breakfast is really important.*
>
> *Teenager: I have to eat all day long!*

> *Parent: You mean there is too much in your lunchbox.*
>
> *Teenager: Yeah, I really can't eat all that. Kylie also only gets two sandwiches a day for school.*

> *Parent: Oh. Is that enough for her?*
>
> *Teenager: Yeah. She is also a lot skinnier.*

> *Parent: You think Kylie is skinnier and you think that is better.*
>
> *Teenager: Yeah. My stomach is way too fat.*

> *Parent: You'd rather have Kylie's stomach?*
>
> *Teenager: Yeah, and her face. I just think I look strange with my face and body.*

> *Parent: So you think you look strange. Are you talking about the way you look, or do you have problems with being adopted, and because your friends aren't?*
>
> *Teenager: That too. I just feel different.*

> *Parent: You feel different to your friends. Yeah, of course you are. I would also find it hard to deal with that. I would be happy to talk to you about that, if you want to. Maybe we can have lunch next week sometime. We'll buy you some new shoes at the same time, what do you think?*

You can also summarise a longer story. Try to be neutral and repeat in your own words whatever you hear. In your summary, you may also want to say something about the active emotions that your child is expressing verbally or non-verbally. Most of the time, a reaction will automatically follow. Your child will nod, or he'll deny or clarify what he said. You might want to ask if you interpreted his story correctly:

> *So you'd rather not celebrate your adoption day, because lately you've been thinking about your brother and sister, who are probably still living with your birth mother in Colombia. You'd rather be with them. (Am I right?)*

You could continue the conversation by giving your own opinion or thoughts about the situation (Step 2):

> *I can well imagine that it isn't nice to know that your brother and sister are still living with your birth mother. It is sad that she was able to take care of them, but not you.*

Now you may want to provide an alternative for the adoption day, an alternative that may suit your child's feelings at that moment:

> *Maybe we can do something else on that day. Something that suits your feelings. Do you have an idea?*

You may want to make a suggestion:

> *Perhaps we can write a letter to the orphanage. We could ask if there are any family pictures that we could have.*

They might have information – you never know.

Try not to take away your teenager's sadness by proposing positive alternatives, or by silencing it. It may give him the feeling that you are rejecting his sadness or anger.

Following up in reaction to subjective words

In practically every sentence, people (unconsciously) convey signals about their feelings. Subjective words in particular reveal a great deal. These are words that are interpreted differently by everyone; for example: 'I feel happy, beautiful, ugly, pretty, angry, sad, strange, crazy.' All these kind of words have a different emotional charge for each individual. Other words that can have many different, personal meanings are, for example: stupid, dark, ugly, light, nice, beautiful, pain, sick, rotten, far, close, later, earlier, hard, easy, cold, warm, real, sad, happy and lovely. In a conversation, these subjective words can be picked out and followed up (if you think necessary). When your teenager says, for example, 'I wish I was normal', you might want to ask him what he means by "normal". In this way you will get a better picture of his emotional world and find out that "normal" probably means something completely different to him than to you. You can also give a confirmation of receipt by repeating the word "normal" or by repeating the whole sentence. You may also ask a direct, open question:

You wish you were normal.

or:

What do you mean by normal?

If your teenager does not respond, you might want to guess neutrally about the reason, so your teenager can respond:

You wish you looked less Asian.

or:

> *You wish you had never been put up for adoption.*

Here is an example of a conversation that starts with naming/identifying behaviour and to which your teenager will respond with subjective words:

> *Parent: Lately you seem uncomfortable with reading books or looking at pictures that have to do with your adoption.*
>
> *Teenager: No. I just hate them.*
>
> *Parent: You hate the pictures.*
>
> *Teenager: Yes, I look so stupid.*
>
> *Parent: What do you mean by stupid?*
>
> *Teenager: I have strange eyes.*
>
> *Parent: Why strange?*
>
> *Teenager: At school, nobody has my eyes.*

From here, you can guide the conversation by naming the actual situation and by asking in an affirmative or questioning way what your teenager's feelings are about the situation:

> *Parent: It is true that nobody in your school has Asian eyes. You would rather have your friend's eyes?*
>
> *Teenager: Yes, that would be very nice.*

Next, you might want to express your own feelings, so you'll validate him:

> *I can imagine that it is not always nice to be different. I think you are beautiful the way you are, but that won't*

help of course. When I was your age, I also always wanted to be like my friends. I feel bad for you that you aren't.

You probably will be tempted to try and get your teenager out of his sombre mood by making a positive statement, but you had better try not to do so. Children (and adults) often interpret positive statements as an indication that their feelings are not being validated. Try to respect your teenager's feelings. Maybe he needs to think about his being different for a while, and maybe it will help to turn his sadness or frustration into something tangible by turning his attention to his adoption history or his birth parents. If your teenager has been able to fully work through his emotions, he probably feels the need himself to give a more positive interpretation of his adoption. However, if he gets stuck in his sombre mood for too long, it might be a good idea to provide him with a more positive or realistic view.

Confronting and "dropping pebbles"

Conversations with adolescents do not always end without confrontations. As a parent, it is important that you stay calm and that your responses are not too much influenced by the intensity of your teenager's reactions. A neutral tone is the most effective and provides your teenager with the most respect. Sometimes it can be helpful to confront your child with his own words. If you do so, it is even more important that you state your position neutrally and do not use an aggressive tone. The fact that you are confronting your teenager is difficult enough for him. If he gets the feeling that you are attacking him, he will get angry or end the conversation.

A good confrontation can be stimulating, in the sense that your teenager will be triggered to think about things and feel invited to respond. Such a confrontation is often a less neutral way of giving a confirmation of receipt or a summary of what he has just said:

So you think it is strange that we adopted you. It would
have been better if we had left you at the orphanage,
because then you would not have felt like a second choice.
If you had been our first choice, it would have been
different. (Am I correct?)

It may seem shocking to bring up such a delicate subject, but it
doesn't necessarily have to be, as long as you *do not use the*
confrontation as an attack, but as a serious means of conversing.
Your teenager will sense your intention and, because of your neutral
tone, will be able to think through his thoughts and feelings. His
own interpretation will be filtered through your summary and as a
result he can better judge whether that was what he really meant.
The conversation might go as follows:

Teenager: I don't know.

Parent: What do you not know?

Teenager: If it would have been different.

Parent: You mean you don't know if it would have mattered
if you were first or second choice.

Teenager: I think I just wouldn't have wanted to be
adopted.

Parent: You mean you would rather have stayed in your birth
country.

Teenager: Yes. With my mother and father. They just
shouldn't have left me.

You might also want to use the technique of confronting your
teenager in a more indirect way by 'dropping pebbles'. According to
van Gulden and Bartels-Rabb (2001, p.200), pebbles are 'one-liners,
not conversations, that raise an issue and then are allowed to ripple
until the child is ready to pick up on it'. By dropping pebbles you are
tempting your child to think about the situation in a different way

without asking for a direct reaction:

> *I have been hearing a lot lately about Chinese children who are reunited with their birth parents. I could imagine that you would also like to try to find your birth parents when you are a little older.*

> *Did you read that interview in the newspaper with that Ukranian boy? I was really touched. That boy had a very similar history to you and told so much about himself. You probably recognised many of his feelings.*

> *You really play the saxophone very beautifully. Maybe your birth mother was musical, too. Or maybe you got that talent from your birth father. I often wonder who gave you that wonderful talent.*

> *I understand that many adopted children find it hard to have been rejected when they were young and that they are often afraid of being rejected again in the future.*

By using this "pebbles technique" you can challenge your teenager in a safe, non-threatening way. The comparison is "out there", without your teenager having to respond. He can let it sink in and come back to it later if he wants to. In fact, through making such a casual remark, you are showing him it is perfectly normal that he wants to know things about his birth parents or that he can be sad, afraid or angry about the adoption, etc.

General advice

- Teenagers want to be raised democratically. They want to be heard and respected. Exchanging opinions is an important factor. Try to allow your teenager to think for himself as much as possible. Teenagers often reach the same conclusion as you would, albeit with a detour. By allowing your teenager to think for himself, you are giving him a certain independence that can help him identify with adulthood, and can help him grow towards it in a safe way.

- If you suspect that your teenager does not have enough basic trust, or if you notice little reaction after asking questions, then it's probably better to stop asking them. Children who have little basic trust are often afraid of answering other people's questions. It may be more productive to simply name your teenager's behaviour, wishes, feelings and thoughts (see Chapter 7). That will make it more likely he will find the courage to share his feelings with you.
- Regularly compliment your teenager. Girls usually like to be complimented more on their personality; they usually want to be liked, while boys prefer to be complimented about some public achievement (Delfos, 2005a, p.146). Indirect compliments work best. For example: 'How were you able to get such a good grade?' This encourages your child to tell you how he did it, which will give him basic trust because he identifies his own strengths and names them (see 'Asking goal-oriented questions' in Chapter 9) (*J/M pubers*, nr. 4 April 2007, 'Zonder mandaat begin je niks').
- If you want to deepen the conversation, it is important to show your teenager that your questions come from a sincere interest. Especially between the ages of 14 and 16, teenagers often create a lot of distance from their parents. Your questioning method may make them feel as if they are being interrogated, which can make them resist talking. For the same reason, it is important to vary your style of questioning.
- Sometimes it is not even necessary to ask direct questions or actively receive with words what your teenager says: active, non-verbal listening can function as a follow-up question. By actively listening, you give your child the feeling that you are sincerely interested in him. This will stimulate him to continue talking. Dropping into silence (but not for too long) can also have the function of a follow-up question: your teenager gets the chance to let his words echo in his mind and this can encourage him to expand on what he said.
- Do not doubt your teenager's words, even though they sound like an overreaction. Follow up on subjective terms; they might give you insight into his personal world.
- If your teenager clearly states that he does not want to discuss something, it is important that you honour his wish. Talk about the

"communication situation":

> *Since we started to talk about your grades, you've constantly been staring out the window. I don't think you want to talk about them. I can see why, it is a difficult subject. But I do want us to talk about this. Have you got a suggestion as to when and how we could do that?*

- "Meta-communication" about your teenager's silence gives him partial responsibility for the conversation ending.
- Meta-communication (talking about the conversational situation) can be very helpful in other situations too, for example, if the conversation is not going too well, if your teenager is caught by his emotions or if you lose the thread of the conversation.

> *I see that you are having a difficult time talking about it. You can hardly hold back your tears. Shall we continue later or do you want to go on?*

> *That phone call interrupted our conversation. Do you remember where we were? I'd like it if we finished that conversation. Do you think that's a good idea?*

> *We are discussing all these things now, but what do you think? Did you want to talk about it in the first place?*

- With older teenagers (16 to 18), it is important that you meta-communicate about the conversation's intention, and about the conditions of equality:

> *I really want to talk to you about this because I think it might help you. But if you want to talk about it later, that's alright of course. Your contribution to this conversation is as important as mine.*

- If you notice that your teenager does not like to talk, it might be that he needs some space. A teenager in a Dutch parenting magazine says:

> I used to be flooded with questions when I got out of school. 'How was your day?' 'Did you get any tests

back?' They were immediately on top of me. When I
left school, I was usually dead tired. I wouldn't even
want to talk, so I hardly answered. Now they let me be
for a while, ask me how I've been around suppertime.
They also trust me more and wait for me to come to
them if something is wrong. In the end I always do, but
only at the moments that I want to. Since I get some
more space from them, I tell them more. I feel better
understood and respected. That's good, because you
won't get there alone.

(Quoted from Dutch parenting magazine: *JIM pubers nr.
4*, April 2007, 'Zonder mandaat begin je niks')

- Adopted children are especially vulnerable to the feeling that they
  are "worthless as a person". Sentences like 'You are so hard to
  handle/obnoxious/tiresome' contain implicit judgements of your
  teenager as a person, while in fact you are only judging his
  behaviour. Try to be as objective as possible by neutrally naming
  what your teenager does and explicitly commenting on that:

  *You are sneaking out. I don't like that. If you do not want
  to stay, just tell me.*

  *You are home late, all the time. You have not been keeping
  your promise for two weeks now. I don't like that. (I am
  worried about you every night, or: I want you to keep your
  promises, as everyone else does in this household).*

- Try to avoid "why" questions and try not to use the words 'you
  need', 'you have to' or 'you must'. A teenager in a Dutch parenting
  magazine says:

  My parents are more focused on my positive sides now.
  On the things that go well. They don't say: 'You have to
  do your homework.' But they ask: 'How is maths
  going?' I like that, because if I have to do something,
  I am less likely to do it. I think: I am the boss. But in this
  way I really do stuff.

Conclusion: the importance of sincere interest, respect and modesty

In the last two chapters, I have discussed several communicative skills that can help to keep the conversation with your teenager going. Although it may at first seem hard to learn these skills, in fact a lot of parents have already learned a lot from "ordinary situations" and are very capable of communicating with their teenagers. Parents who are genuinely interested in their child are especially good at automatically responding sensitively and responsively, by taking a sincere interest and respecting the child's thoughts and wishes, and by being modest enough to set their own wishes, thoughts and feelings aside. This combination of elements usually leads to an active listening role for the parent, and to good questions to ask. There's a good chance you are intuitively doing things right. If, however, you and/or your teenager are going through a difficult time, it may be useful to sharpen up these communicative skills and become aware of the effect of certain responses. At these moments, the communicative skills discussed in Chapter 7 can be of use. It is very likely that you will be able to get communication going again in this way. It is important that you remain sincere, respectful and modest during these conversations.

In the next and final chapter, I specifically discuss talking about adoption and show how your teenager's adoption-related thoughts can be recognised and how you can talk about them.

9

Talking about adoption: helping to change thoughts

[...] Imagine what it would have been like if they had just said: 'Daniel, we suspect that the way you're feeling now has something to do with your adoption. Would you like to talk about it?' A depression is often caused by an unfinished grieving process. Some adopted children talk of a deep-rooted sadness that seems to be constant and seems to infiltrate everything; an obstacle in the way of real enjoyment. Not knowing why you are grieving as an adopted child only makes processing your feelings harder.
Daniel (age 20), Colombia

Introduction

As you have read in previous chapters, adopted children are particularly vulnerable during puberty. Many of their thoughts and feelings can be the result of their history: 'Who are my birth parents? Do I look like them? Do I have brothers and sisters? Why did they not want me? Was something wrong with me?' Because identity development is crucial during this period, they now need "real", solid answers more than ever. Moreover, due to their rapid cognitive development, children also become more fully aware of the fact that they have been relinquished. Feeling "worthless" or "given up" can start to play an important role in how they feel and behave.

It is obvious that your child will want to repress these painful feelings. After all, living with this knowledge and the pain that causes it cannot be much fun. The result may be, however, that your teenager (unconsciously) hides her feelings behind a mask of anger or rage, that she becomes depressive or extremely fearful or develops an eating disorder, or that she seeks an escape in an addiction.

To prevent this, it is important that you are alert to the growing and continuously changing understanding that your teenager has of her adoption so that you can respond to it at appropriate moments. If you are able to react suitably to your teenager's behaviour, she will feel safe with you and there's a good chance that she will dare to accept the pain that accompanies adoption. This will make it possible for her to connect herself with her past. This connection is necessary if she is to stop being alone and begin forming new, deeply rooted bonds with others.

In Chapter 7, I showed you the importance of reacting sensitively and responsively. If you can name/identify the feelings and behaviour of your teenager in an appropriate way, she will develop basic trust and talk more easily about her thoughts and feelings. In Chapter 8, I discussed techniques for asking follow-up questions in a sensitive and responsive way. The skills learned in Chapters 7 and 8 can be important, especially when communication gets stuck and an open conversation seems impossible. In this last chapter I want, above all, to discuss how to recognise and deal with the unrealistic, automatic thoughts that your teenager may have developed as a result of adoption. In addition to this, I once again deal with adoption-related grief and the "healthy" and "unhealthy" emotions that can result from it. I discuss how you can handle unhealthy emotions and also consider certain positive questions that might help your teenager to break through a certain impasse of feelings. I end the chapter with some advice that will help you to create openness and trust.

The influence of automatic thoughts

Every person has thoughts and feelings. According to RET (rational emotive therapy), there is a causal link between the two: to a significant extent, thoughts determine our feelings. To be able to feel differently, RET says, it is important to change your way of thinking. (RET was developed by the psychotherapist Albert Ellis, and is one of the most widely applied and popular forms of therapy in the United States and Europe. See Verhulst, 2005.) The basic hypothesis of RET is that problems are mostly caused by the way we look at the things that happen to us. This explains why two people can experience the same situation in very different ways. Someone who fails a test can react in various ways:

- I knew it, I can't do it. I'm not going to pass the re-sit either. Gosh, how will I tell my friends? I am so ashamed. I am worthless.
- Ah, damn. And I thought I was doing alright. Now I'll have to take the re-sit. Well, I'll just see how that goes. Otherwise I will just do the last year again. This last year was a good one anyway and I'll be in class with my friend Nicky again.
- See, I thought so. They really made the exam hard this year, that's really unfair. They changed it just when I had to take the test. Because they did that, I'll have to do the re-sit. And that's going to be just as hard.
- Oh, how horrible. This is the worst thing that could have happened to me. Everyone passed and I failed. I am never going to recover.

Negative thoughts often lead to negative feelings and positive thoughts lead to more positive feelings. Why one person is more positive than another depends on many factors. Someone who is by nature an optimist is more likely to handle something more positively than someone who is mainly pessimistic or melancholic. The way one views situations can also be the result of one's history/circumstances, the parenting situation, the amount of basic trust that she has been able to build up, etc (see also Chapter 1).

Under the influence of all these factors, every child develops different basic thoughts about herself at a young age. These basic thoughts can influence how someone feels as a child. This means that children from early on can think that they are talented, sociable, smart, like dad, etc. They can also start thinking that they are always fighting, bad at maths, egotistical, incapable of doing anything, etc. From these automatic thoughts, children start judging themselves – and when they get closer to adulthood, these thoughts will start playing a comparatively prominent role in their development. A structurally negative or fearful feeling will often result from certain basic thoughts that the child developed when she was young.

Because of their history, adopted children often develop negative basic thoughts at a young age. They may have started thinking that they are not worth anything, always have to be sweet, etc. I explain this below.

Automatic thoughts as a result of the adoption

Because of their history, adopted children often tend to develop unrealistic automatic thoughts. Children who have gone through a lot of difficulties in their country of birth are especially likely to have developed thoughts that were probably realistic then, but have lost their usefulness now. But adopted children who cannot remember anything of what happened to them also develop unrealistic basic thoughts about themselves, for example, when they start to realise that they have been relinquished or that they are different. In Chapters 3–6, I have discussed several automatic thoughts that can influence adopted teenagers. Unrealistic basic thoughts, which can be developed at a young age, might be:

- I always have to be nice, otherwise I will be sent away.
- I have to show that I am alright.
- I have to be nice or I will not be chosen.
- I am worthless because my parents hit/left/neglected me.
- I am worthless because I was thrown away like a doll.
- I am worthless because my adoptive parents would rather have their own birth child.
- I must not have been sweet enough as a toddler because I was not allowed to stay (and my brothers and sisters were).
- I am not pretty/healthy enough, so I was given up.
- It would be better if I did not start loving someone because I will be left in the end.
- I will be alone again soon (when I leave the house I will be left again).
- I am different and will never fit in.
- I look like my birth parents, there is nothing I can do about it (I have inherited bad genes).
- I have no right to exist because my parents didn't want me.
- I will never escape the social class I was born into.
- My birth parents were bad people so I must be a bad person.
- I have to be grateful that my adoptive parents saved me.
- I should not yearn for my birth parents because they were bad people.
- I have to be loyal and nice to my adoptive parents or I will lose them too.
- I cannot be curious about my past because, if I am, I will be rejecting my adoptive parents.

Some of these thoughts may have been functional in the past – their purpose was "survival". It can be very helpful for young children to think that they should be nice or else they will be rejected. Every child needs warmth and love and if they want to get that they should behave themselves. The thought that they have to be grateful to their adoptive parents can be useful sometimes. If they behave gratefully towards their parents, they have the best chance of receiving love and affection from them. Even negative thoughts like 'I am different and will never fit in', or 'I am worthless' come from a functional survival mechanism: by thinking that no one loves you, you are protecting yourself from (more) future harm. Both extremes are the result of the same need for love and the same fear of rejection.

Becoming aware of these automatic thoughts can help adopted teenagers. They can understand that their thoughts are *not* reality, but only an interpretation of reality – and that this interpretation is the result of their experiences in the past. This will also allow them to learn that, in the here and now, other, new explanations and thoughts can be created, and that these can influence their feelings and behaviour positively.

Helping to change automatic thoughts

Changing automatic thoughts is not as easy as it might seem. They are often deeply buried in the human brain, and therefore in your teenager's brain too. This is mainly because these thoughts enable her to have the feeling that she understands the world and that these thoughts can help her from being hurt or abandoned again. In other words, automatic thoughts give your child a sense of knowing what she is up against – and that is a safe feeling.

Because adolescents are more open to different sorts of information than young children and adults, and because they like to investigate their own world view and self-image, it is during this period that you will probably be best able to help your child investigate her thoughts. Adolescents are nosy, fair and open to surprising new perspectives. Instead of giving compliments (which probably don't work any more), you can probably better talk with her about her ways of thinking. Is what she thinks the "real and realistic truth"? When she becomes aware that her thoughts do *not* represent reality but are only a personal view of it, she may be able to let in other, more realistic thoughts, which may help her to feel different.

For this to work, it is important that you create a safe environment for your teenager. According to Heffels (2006, p.76), there are

certain basic requirements for the development of healthy
(productive) thoughts. (I have expressed Heffels' conditions in my
own words and applied them to suit adopted children specifically.)
Children should at least:

- be safely bonded (so they will be able to engage in healthy
  relationships);
- feel sufficiently autonomous (so they will dare to know themselves);
- have built up enough frustration tolerance (so they will be able to
  work things out and change negative thoughts around);
- feel free to express their emotions and needs (so they will not have
  to behave socially acceptably and can explore their true feelings and
  show them);
- feel there is enough room for spontaneity and play (so they will not
  be too harsh on themselves and will not think in absolute truths).

This last basic need is important insofar as children who are not
allowed enough room for spontaneity and play are prone to
perfectionism and thus to having "absolute thoughts" where words
like "never", "always", "again", "have to", etc, play an important
role. These absolute thoughts are especially likely to form the basis
for unrealistic, automatic thoughts. They leave little room for other
interpretations. In a conversation with your teenager, you may want
to take the following four steps:

1. Search for automatic thoughts (using Polderman's model and
   following up; see Chapters 7 and 8).
2. Ask about the facts underlying such thoughts (for example: 'What
   are your reasons for believing that? Is that always true? What is it
   exactly you are scared for? What could happen? Does this thought
   remind you of the past?').
3. Talk about the usefulness of such a thought ('Is that thought
   realistic? What does that thought do for you? What do you feel like
   when you think those thoughts? Does that thought help you in any
   way? How did that thought help you in the past?'). It is especially
   important that your teenager starts to understand that her
   automatic thoughts may have been realistic in the past, but aren't

any longer. As a result, she may also start to become more aware of the adoption-related pain that is behind these automatic thoughts.

4. Formulate new and helpful thoughts. You can do this by summarising what your teenagers has said in Step 3 above, and then asking your teenager for her opinion again:

> *So you are reluctant to leave home because you will than be alone again, just as you were when you birth parents left you. You think you will be just as lonely. And while we are talking, you possibly have started to realise that these thoughts aren't as realistic as they were before, because we have been together for 15 years: our connection is unbreakable, it will always exist. You know that you have friends who are always there for you, that you can always call them or us and that you are free to come and sleep over here if you want. What thoughts might help you better?*

If your teenager becomes aware of the fact that her feelings are influenced by automatic thoughts and that she used them in the past for self-protection, she can learn to feel the pain associated with them. She can, at the same time, learn to be less influenced by these thoughts now. However, it is important that you do not take on the role of therapist. If you start interpreting her behaviour, it will have a boomerang effect on the relationship you have with your child. The best help you can give her, as a parent, is to listen carefully to her words and observe her behaviour well. If everything is alright, your sensitive and active way of listening and questioning will set your teenager thinking (see Chapter 7 and 8) and that, in the end, is what it is all about. A conversation might go as follows.

> **Teenager: Sam broke up with me.**
>
> *Parent: Really? How terrible. You look pretty hurt. When did he do that?*

Teenager: Yesterday, he sent me an email.

Parent: By email? I can imagine that hurts even more.

Teenager: Oh, it doesn't really matter.

Parent: What do you mean? Aren't you hurt?

Teenager: Well, yeah, of course I am. But it's better if I'm not all dramatic about it.

Parent: You'd rather not be dramatic. I would be really shook up if it happened to me. You were seeing each other for almost a year now! An email is not a very nice way to break up with you.

Teenager: Maybe it's better that he didn't say it to my face. He won't see how shocked I am now.

Parent: You'd rather not have him see how hurt you are.

Teenager: I'm not hurt. I'm shocked, I said.

Parent: You are shocked about Sam breaking up with you, but you aren't sad.

Teenager: No, I am not going to let myself get hurt by this. I'll just get over the shock and get on with life. I am not going to lie awake over this.

Parent: You'd rather not be sad.

Teenager: No. I was sad when I was little.

Parent: You mean when we came to get you in Ethiopia?

Teenager: Yes. When my mother gave me up.

Parent: Yes, that was very sad too. Your mother gave you up after you'd lived with her for six years. That must have hurt incredibly.

Silence. Daughter looks out of the window.

> *Teenager: You know. I really wanted to be his girlfriend. I really didn't want him to break up with me.*
>
> *Parent: I understand. You really loved Sam. You were a great couple. It's only natural that you're sad about him breaking up with you.*
>
> *Teenager: Yeah, but I don't want to feel that way any more.*
>
> *Parent: You don't want to feel sad because it reminds you of the past too much, when you had to say goodbye to your mother.*

Daughter nods, stares at the ground.

> *Parent: If you are all alone and there is no one to comfort you, I can imagine that you do not want to feel sad. That might have been a wise decision long ago, but is that thought really still useful now?*
>
> *Teenager: No.*

Daughter swallows.

> *Parent: You know. That thought, not wanting to feel sad, may have helped you a lot in the past. Now you've got us and a couple of very good friends who all want to comfort you. I am sure they will all understand.*

Daughter cries.

> *Teenager: I just really, really loved Sam.*
>
> *Parent: That's what it looked like. You really loved him. I think it was really courageous of you to dare to love him so much, even though you knew that you might lose him, like*

your mother. And I am really sorry that you two broke up.
Shall I run you a bath?

It is important that you only start a conversation about your
teenager's adoption if she really wants to. If she feels safe and has
developed enough basic trust, she will start talking about it herself
when she is ready. The most important thing is that you are honest
and truthful with her, and that you provide the conditions for her
to take the initiative. You can, for example, actively name that your
teenager looks sad. Whether she elaborates or not should be up
to her.

If your teenager often expresses explicit, absolute thoughts, it is
important that you make her aware of this. Very explicit thoughts
are mostly not very realistic and therefore not very productive. The
best thing you can do is to follow up on subjective terms like
"always", "never", "have to", etc (see 'Following up in reaction to
subjective words' in Chapter 8). In this way, you are questioning the
facts behind her automatic thoughts.

> **Teenager: I'm never lucky. I'm always being pushed
> aside.**
>
> *Parent: You think you're never lucky in life. You have had a
> lot of trouble with your friends lately, haven't you? But is it
> really true that you are always being pushed aside?*
>
> **Teenager: Yes.**
>
> *Parent: Even by Stacey, your best friend?*
>
> **Teenager: Well, not by her, but by everyone else.**
>
> *Parent: But your best friend would not push you aside.*
>
> **Teenager: No, just as well.**
>
> *Parent: Is that important to you?*

Teenager: Yes, otherwise I'd have no one.

Parent: But you do have someone; in fact, you have a very good friend who would never push you aside. I think that's really something.

Teenager: Yeah, that's true. Maybe I'm just overreacting. Sometimes it just feels like everyone is always pushing me aside.

Parent: Where does that thought come from, do you think?

Teenager: I don't know. I just sometimes feel less important than others.

Parent: You feel less important than others. Are you?

Teenager: I don't think so. It's just a feeling I always have.

Parent: You say that you always have that feeling. But since when?

Daughter shrugs her shoulders

Teenager: I have just always felt different. Even when I was really small. I felt different than other children.

Parent: Because you looked different?

Teenager: Yeah, I was just always different than all the other kids.

Parent: And you've still got that feeling, and that's why you're feeling pushed aside.

Teenager: Something like that. I'm just different and you're the first to go if you're different.

Parent: Except for your best friend.

Teenager: Yeah.

Parent: I can imagine that you felt different before. Little children can be really mean. You can't really trust your best friend then. But you're not little any more and you can trust your best friend now. At least, that's what you said.

Teenager: True. Maybe I'm just overreacting. I also have other friends who always help me, Jessica and Lola.

Now or at some other time, you could continue the conversation by talking about the automatic thoughts of "feeling different" and "feeling rejected". If she understands that these automatic thoughts are the result of her adoption history, she will understand that she may have been rejected at that time, but that now she has friends and parents who will make sure she is not alone. You might explore new, more realistic basic thoughts so your teenager will be able to let go of the feelings she had as a small child.

If your teenager never seems to want to talk and/or consistently behaves in an extreme way, you may want to contact an adoption support worker.

Dealing with adoption-related grief

As I wrote in Chapter 2, under 'Adoption-related grief', most teenagers start thinking more about their history and start feeling more pain about having been relinquished. As a result, most teenagers will work through a grieving process during this period in their lives. A "healthy" grieving process is accompanied by emotions like anger and sadness. Although these are not pleasant emotions, it is better that they are not denied – they help your child to connect with the people and events in the past and present in a healthy way. If the sadness or anger about the adoption is repressed, your teenager's emotions can result in extreme aggression or depression. In the following paragraphs, I discuss certain healthy and unhealthy grieving emotions (I have partially based my research on Verhulst,

2005). When you learn to see the difference, you will be better able to judge what state your teenager is in and if you might need help from an adoption support worker.

Recognising healthy grieving emotions

Healthy grieving emotions are emotions that, even though they are not pleasant, can help someone to move on. They are the result of realistic basic thoughts. Examples of healthy grieving emotions are sadness and anger. In adopted teenagers these feelings are the result of realistic basic thoughts like:

> *I was left and that really hurt. I can feel sad about that for days on end. But I do understand that it was not easy for my birth parents. They had no money and could not feed me.*

Or:

> *I can get so angry when I think about my birth parents. Why did they leave me? That question can keep puzzling me for hours; I don't know a thing. Oh well. There might come a day when I get to know the whole story. Maybe it will turn out that they had a good reason for giving me up and that they think of me often. I'll hold on to those thoughts.*

Healthy grieving emotions are dealt with in the here and now in a pure way, without losing sight of reality in the long run. They teach your teenager to connect with what is important to her, but at the same time to keep in mind that there is more than only this emotion, that people and events are not black or white and that "absolute truths" do not exist.

Recognising unhealthy grieving emotions

Unhealthy grieving emotions are the result of "absolute" basic
thoughts that are not connected to reality. In the long run, they
have a suffocating effect and can lead to apathy. Examples of
unhealthy grieving emotions can be depression, fury, guilt and
shame. In adopted teenagers, these feelings are the result of
unrealistic, automatic thoughts such as:

> *My mother should never have given me up. I will never get
> over this. Life is not worth living to me.*

> *My father should never have left my mother. How did he
> ever think he could get away with that? I really never want
> to see him again. If he even knocks on my door, I will blow
> his brains out.*

> *I am worthless. Who wants a one-armed child? I have been
> maimed for life and that is why nobody loves me.*

> *Why did this all have to happen to me? It's always me, isn't
> it? Others always have more luck than I do.*

> *Everyone is always so critical of me. I am not going to
> listen to their criticism any more. I have figured out for
> myself that I am worthless.*

> *If people are critical of me, they can go screw themselves. I
> cannot deal with people who will not accept me as I am.
> That really pisses me off.*

> *All that whining about adoption... I do not have any
> problems with my adoption and I am sure I will never feel
> the urge to go look for my birth parents.*

In the long run, unhealthy grieving emotions will result in your
teenager talking herself down more and more. Because these

thoughts are absolute and black and white, they are almost never constructive.

If your teenager is often bothered by such unhealthy grieving emotions, the best thing you can do is to teach her to think about these stubborn feelings out loud (see the example conversation in 'Helping to change automatic thoughts' above). What are these feelings based on? If you do this with a pure and sincere intention, your teenager will not feel attacked and she will ultimately get to know herself better. There's a good chance that she is not as aware of her own negative position as you are. Ask her what makes her feel this way. Help her to discover that reality is more varied and more complex. Perhaps she will understand that she will be happier if she changes the way she thinks. The best outcome will be that she learns that she is responsible for her own happiness and that anger and sadness about her adoption are justified emotions, but that fury, frustration, shame or irritation will not help her.

Reality and providing a context

Both RET and the constructive, goal-oriented approach agree on the idea that it is not the problem itself that matters but rather the way you look at it and (re)construct your world accordingly. Research shows, for example, that people are best helped to get over their sombre thoughts when they are able to look further than the particular moment, so they realise that the sadness or anger they are feeling will also pass. Someone who is capable of judging realistically and rationally will be able to experience healthier emotions than someone who can only think of events as black and white and who fails to see the context in which they occur.

The ways in which your teenager thinks and perceives will, to a large extent, define the way she feels about her adoption. Strong feelings of denial, sadness and anger about her adoption history can at times be very functional, especially because in this way she will learn to connect to the world around her. If, however, your teenager keeps circling around in her unhealthy grieving emotions like fury, frustration, aggression, depression or shame, it will not be good for her development. It is important that your teenager gets a better view of reality. You can provide her with this by naming her unhealthy basic thoughts and consequently giving them a positive direction ('Positively prompting' – see Chapter 7) and asking for a confirmation of receipt:

> *Parent: You're thinking: I can't help it because I'm like my dad and he was always picking fights.*
>
> *Teenager: Well, wasn't he?*
>
> *Parent: Your father often fought, yes. I can imagine that you think you are like him. After all, you are his child. But you have to realise that your father was living under completely different circumstances. He spent his whole life on the streets and was never able to know how it feels to be loved by someone. If you haven't learned how it feels to be loved, you haven't learned that you can resolve differences of opinion in nice ways, too. He just didn't know how to handle such things. If he had been raised in a family that had more opportunities, like you, he would have learned that, and he possibly wouldn't have picked fights so often. If he had still wanted to fight, he could have joined a judo club or joined the police force. What are you thinking when you hear these things?*

You may also want to actively search for information to provide your child with a context and reality by showing her documentaries, films or books concerning the political and socio-cultural situation in her country of birth. Stories of other adopted children or other parents who had to give up their child for adoption can give an adopted child a better idea of her own history and thereby a more realistic view of her adoption.

If your teenager is stuck in an unhealthy feeling or is sad or angry for a long period of time, it may help to talk with her about future possibilities so that she can place her feelings in a broader context: she feels very sombre now, but whenever she goes out to do sports with her best friend, she feels less sombre. Her feeling is not a constant one. You may also want to make her realise that she will, at a later time, start viewing her adoption differently. Her feeling now is not an unchangeable, life-long condition and it might help your teenager to realise this. Your teenager might have had periods before in which she thought a lot about her birth parents. If you want to, you can refer to these periods; she probably experienced the fact that those times also passed. Tell her that it can be very painful to lose someone, but that doesn't mean you will never be happy again. This will give your teenager, in a sense, an anchor that she can throw to the future, and she might get some comfort from the idea that she will feel differently some day. In the end, she might even be able to change her absolute thoughts to more realistic thoughts. Do not forget, however, to specifically handle her feelings first.

Showing universality

Your teenager's thoughts will also be put into context if she gets to understand that she is not the only one with those specific feelings. If, for example, she can share her feelings with young people who have similar feelings (through adopted friends, email groups, adoption forums, internet, talking sessions), that might help her to feel less isolated. By sharing similar thoughts and feelings, your teenager will learn to understand herself better and learn to see the universality of her situation. Through a conversation with other adopted children, she may, for example, discover that she is not the only one who longs for her birth parents or feels guilty towards her adoptive parents. She may also discover that, although her own story is unique, the problems are often the same for other adopted children:

I joined a general email group of adopted children, so not specifically other adopted children from India, my birth country. First I thought that it might have been better if I had joined a specifically Indian group, but after a short while I noticed that chatting with adopted children with completely different stories was actually very liberating. I noticed that we all thought about our birth parents and that it did not much matter how long we had been with our birth parents or what we had been through. A world opened before my eyes. Suddenly I was able to talk about my innermost feelings. It was just like looking in a great big mirror. And that happened even though I only knew these other adopted children for a short while. A couple of older adopted people also contributed. That was really nice. They told me that it would start feeling different in a couple of years. That gave me something to hold on to.

Besides contacting others who are in the same position, your teenager can also discover the universality of her feelings by reading books on adoption-related themes. These books do not necessarily have to be about adopted children. They can also be about teenagers who have gone through similar problems because they lost their parents, or because they feel lost or lonely, are different, abused, living in a foster home, have two identities, have a stepfather they cannot get along with, etc.

It can also help if your teenager reads books in which the protagonist is someone who overcomes problems. Even if the problems are only somewhat similar to hers (for example, if they deal with themes like loneliness, feeling left out, etc), your child will not only feel less lonely but will simultaneously be able to identify with the hero in a story and learn how to play a different role in her own life. You can look for books for teenagers that deal with similar questions.

Asking goal-oriented questions

If your child is stuck in negative emotions and thoughts, it may be useful to think about her automatic thoughts and to help her to replace those thoughts with other ones, as I have described above. Sometimes, however, it can be helpful if your child is not too preoccupied with these negative thoughts at all. You can help her to fix her gaze on things that are going on right now and which can provide her with more space and possibilities. By using this "constructive, goal-oriented method" you can, through specific miracle/future questions or descriptive questions (see below), change your teenager's experience of reality positively. Goal-oriented questions are focused on discovering other aspects of reality and bringing out the (often unconsciously active) powers inside your child. If they are asked in accordance with the Socratic method (see Chapter 8), they might enable your teenager to (re-) discover her own possibilities. By noticing these, taking them and underlining them, your child will be able to see her life's more positive storyline. (In my application of several goal-oriented questioning techniques, I have based my research on Parton and O'Byrne, 2000. Their book discusses several ways of using a goal-oriented approach, in which the therapist, by way of questioning, tries to look at the chances and possibilities, instead of the causes of the problem.)

Of course, it is important that your teenager has the feeling that her problems have been validated first. You will then have to find a balance between talking about her problem/feelings first and finding solutions and possibilities for change.

The miracle or future question

The miracle question, or future question, is an attempt at tapping into your teenager's fantasy. Although it may seem illogical to start fantasising, the miracle question can prove to be a powerful tool in helping your child to look at the future in a specific way, and to help find words for what it is that they would like to accomplish. You could ask:

Imagine waking up tomorrow with your problem gone.
You were adopted, but you had no trouble with it at all.
What would be the first thing that would make you realise
that this had happened?

This question might get your child to start making a different future
plan. She can think about what the first signs of change might be,
and by starting to talk about them, create a new reality. In a sense,
you are making a start on her own film, in which she plays the lead
role (with no problems) and of which she is also the director. From
here you can start following up on details about what will happen,
what different family members and friends will say, how different
people will notice the differences and what this will mean to her,
etc. In this way, the solution is assembled without (again) naming
the problem or talking about what can be done to change it. This
new way of describing, where behaviour is stressed instead of what
is felt, can be very liberating. It can be the beginning of a new,
realistic view that will make change possible through a constructive,
goal-oriented method.

If fantasising does not appeal to your teenager, you may also ask
her a (more realistic) future question. This question can do
essentially the same thing:

Imagine that your problems will be much less severe in a
year or two, when you have solved them through hard
work. What changes would we notice about you?

Other miracle and future questions are:

Imagine that you met your birth parents. What would that
change for you? What would we notice about you?

What if tomorrow we would be able to get along? What
would be the first thing that would make you realise that?

*What would you say? How would we react? How would
others notice that this had happened?*

The idea behind this way of questioning is that if your child is able
to imagine and talk about a more positive, problem-free future, a
reality is created that will enhance the chances of it actually
happening. Imagining a better future can be an important step
towards change. This goal-oriented, constructive approach can be
a very important power tool (Parton and O'Byrne, 2000, p.103).

Keep in mind that future questions or miracle questions have to be,
to some extent, realistic. Imagining that the person was not adopted
is not realistic, because it will never be the case. These questions are
most useful when the future is imminent, for example, tomorrow:

*What would I see you do tomorrow if you suddenly had a
lot of confidence?*

What would we notice?

What would we say?

How would you feel about that?

According to the solution-based approach, "doing-as-if" is almost
the same as doing. Your child is, in fact, practising her new
behaviour, without having to do much for it. You should realise that
it sometimes takes time and that several conversations might be
necessary to think up new possibilities for your child. Not every child
is immediately ready to face the future.

The "worth-the-trouble" question
This question is supplementary to the miracle and future questions,
but is aimed specifically at the conversation itself. By asking about
the positive outcome of the conversation, you can get to know

what it is your child wants to accomplish if she has a good feeling about it:

What would be a good outcome of the conversation for you? What would you like to accomplish?

Imagine that you left our conversation with the feeling that it had really been worthwhile to talk. What would have happened in our conversation?

What would make you feel good about the outcome of the conversation? What would have been discussed or happened?

The scale question

With scale questions, you are building a bridge with your child, a way to talk about subjects that are otherwise hard to describe. A scale question is a question that, through grading the scale of the problem, lets your child decide how bad the problem is for her, and how badly she would like to see the problem solved. Doing this means that the problem is given a value that will help to make the steps toward improvement more tangible, for example (examples from Parton and O'Byrne, 2000, p.104):

If 0 is the start and 10 complete success, where would you say you are on the scale? Where would you want to end up? How would you notice that you had gone up the scale?

If 0 means that you are doubting and 10 means that you are sure you want to solve the problem, where are you now? How would you notice that you had gone up the scale?

If 1 stands for your sadness about failing your test last

month, and 10 would mean your sadness is all gone, where would you say you are on the scale now?

Scale questions define more precisely how your child would grade her position or what your child would be doing to work up the scale:

How different would your life look if you went from a 5 to a 6 on the scale?

What makes it a 3?

In this way you may be able to help your child to accomplish change. Moving up one point on the scale is often more than enough. By taking it slowly, your teenager will, in the end, move faster. Successes will be more easily gained. This will probably motivate her to change faster in the end.

The exception-finding or description question

Questions aimed at finding exceptions are often able to activate the problem-solving capacities of the listener. They take for granted that things don't always happen in the same way and that there are always exceptions to be found. These exceptions often shelter the seeds of solutions and can be revived by naming them as important events (Parton and O'Byrne, 2000, p.100). By showing your child the one moment when she did feel good, and by asking how she brought that feeling about, she may realise that this situation can be repeated, and that she can influence it. Questions that look for exceptions are, for example:

Are there moments when you do not feel sad/different? When is that? At what kinds of occasions? What do you do to make you feel happier/less different? What do others do to make you feel happier/less different? How do you respond to others? How do others respond to you?

Are there any friends who would not leave you? Are there friends who are nice to you? Who are they? What do you do to those friends so they are nice to you? What do they do to you? Are those friends similar to one another, or are they all different? What makes them different?

Exception-finding questions always ask for a description. The more detailed a description is, the more tangible the reasons become for reacting in a certain way or feeling differently. Even if your child is sad or angry about a definite loss (for example, of her birth parents), if she is stuck in her sadness, it can help her to think about other moments of loss and how she dealt with them. Descriptive questions often asked are:

And what more?

How did you deal with that?

How did you get over that?

How did you deal with that situation?

What is the difference between this and that time?

Why did it not become worse then?

Observation assignments can also be a useful way of finding exceptions:

Try to be aware of the moments when you are very happy. I want to know what is different then. What do you do differently? What do others do differently?

Count the times that you repress your anger. What do you do, to be able to do it? What do others do when you succeed?

Try to catch your teacher when he isn't picking on you. Write down what you were doing differently then.

Try to observe what your teacher/your friends were doing when you noticed they care about you and try to help you.

Try to observe when you are feeling good and when you don't feel different in school and among your friends. What do you do to make it different? What do others do differently?

Write down everything that happened in your life that you like or that you would like to keep that way. (By writing down what does not have to change, it can become clear what does.)

If your child insists that there are no exceptions and she is stuck in the "impossibility or problem mode", she may not be ready to think about solutions. The best thing you can do then is to act sensitively and responsively, that you validate her problems and feelings. Now (or later, in a different conversation) you can rely on the miracle question (see above). What would it be like if the problem ceased to exist? If your child is open to this and talks about it, it will be accepted into her positive fantasies and, as a result, she may be able to recall exceptions, although she thought she wasn't able to before (Parton and O'Byrne, 2000, pp.106–7).

Creating openness: advice

In the above section, I have focused on several questioning and conversational approaches that can help you and your teenager accomplish a more constructive dialogue on adoption. In this last section, I would like to give some advice that can help create openness; these advices do not immediately relate to a certain questioning method or conversational technique.

Taking feelings seriously

Take your teenager's emotions about her adoption seriously and try to impose your own feelings as little as possible (see Chapter 6). Try not to stress the fact that she has to "move on". Someone who is grieving needs space to show her feelings. Support her and help her where you can; daring to grieve is hard work. If you validate her thoughts and feelings, she will, in most cases, get over her sombre or sad mood.

Connecting with the past

If your teenager is allowed to grieve, she will learn to connect with the past. While grieving, she will possibly learn not to be afraid of her sadness because it has everything to do with love and the acknowledgement of the fact that she has lost something precious as a young child and that she, as a result, felt very scared and lonely. If she can connect with whatever she has lost, she will be better able to shape her relationships in the future. In the end, loss is mainly a question of staying connected, not of letting go.

Letting your teenager explore for herself

Allow your teenager not to talk about her adoption if she wishes. It is important that she discovers her own feelings and is able to express them herself. Every person is different and handles emotions differently. What you *can* do is to give her the chance to talk about it if she wants to, by using the "pebbles technique", for example (see Chapter 8). The most important thing is that you are sensitive and responsive to her development. It is important that she decides when to tell what she feels and what impact this has on her. Sometimes, it can be helpful to provide your child with a structure for her emotions, for example, if she is drowning in her sombre feelings. You can provide this structure by providing a context and reality for her thoughts, or by focusing her attention on a different, more positive reality (see 'Reality and providing a context', 'Showing universality' and 'Asking goal-oriented questions', above).

Holding back painful information

Be sure that you are not keeping any painful information from your child. It is important for the development of a teenager's identity that (at the very start of adolescence or, even better, before) she has all the information at hand. She can only feel safe with you if she is sure that you are not keeping important information from her. If you have doubts about telling certain things because it may be too painful, or because your teenager may not be able to handle it, contact an adoption support worker. Do not postpone it. It is better for your child to receive negative information than no information at all (see 'I want to spare my child the sadness and pain over his past' in Chapter 6). In Chapter 4 of *Adoption Conversations: What, when and how to tell* (written for parents with adopted or foster children from 0–12 years old) I have written down several scenarios that can help you share painful information. These scenarios might allow you to shape more of your child's background information.

You should realise that children are often relieved to know the complete truth. They are often bothered by missing information; they seem older or younger or they have to keep guessing at the reasons for being given up. Sometimes children dream of meeting their parents, when in fact they are dead, or for years they think that the information is worse than it really is:

> My parents were fairly open about my adoption, but always silent about my father. They told me that he left my mother when I was young, and that this was the main reason for adoption. I fantasised about my father for years. What had he done to make my parents hush things up? Did he rape my mother? Was he an addict or a criminal? Was I born out of an incestuous

> relationship? When I was 19 and was about to leave
> home, my mother confided in me. She wanted to tell
> me something about my father. I was really nervous.
> Then she told me that he had been a very sweet man,
> but had died five days after my birth. They had kept it
> silent because they thought that I would have been sad
> if I had known. The opposite happened.
> I started glowing inside. I turned out to have a father to
> be proud of! If only they had told me before.

Even if you have to tell your child painful things about her birth
parents, it is likely that she will be relieved to know. She has
probably been (unconsciously) plagued by vague and fearful
memories and will probably feel validated emotionally when she
hears how things really went. She will suddenly be able to
understand her fearful or uncertain feelings and may feel very
supported by knowing the truth.

When giving information, keep in mind that certain information
in the adoption file may not be genuine. It is, for example, not
necessarily the case that the parents of foundlings are unknown. It
may be that the parents are known, but not named in the file. They
may also become known in later years, without you knowing it. For
example, Chinese children are not always given up because of the
one-child policy. They may be children born as a result of
extramarital affairs or given up out of poverty, sickness or the
death of a parent. If later on you decide to look for the facts, new
information is bound to come to light. It is important that when you
share the information with your teenager, you are aware of this.
Make sure your child knows that the information in the adoption
file might not be complete or genuine.

Clarifying the reason for adoption
One of the most important questions for an adopted child is the
question why they were given up. Questions like: 'Was I wanted?'
and 'Did my parents love me?' are often more important to them

than the fact that they were adopted. Especially the knowledge *that they weren't just done away with* is important for their self-image:

> I always felt that I was born a mistake. I thought that if they – my birth parents – didn't want to keep me then I had to have been a mistake. I was not worthy to be here. My birth mum didn't want me, my birth dad didn't want me. Those words kept pounding my brain.
>
> Then something incredible happened to me. I pushed my parents in therapy to get me more information about my birth parents. My therapist helped me with this. My parents were really nervous about what I would find. We called the agency where I was adopted from and I found out that my birth mum tried to parent me for four months – she really did care about me!! She cared enough to try to keep me; the records said that she tried but eventually found it was too hard to raise me by herself. For fourteen years I believed I was a mistake! Providing me with some of the missing information allowed me to no longer see myself as a kid that was not wanted!
> (from Riley, 2005, pp.120–1)

If your teenager wants to, try to find as much information as possible about why she was adopted. If there is no information at all, the best thing you can do is develop realistic scenarios. You can make use of political, cultural and social information known about the country of birth at the time of her adoption. Also keep in mind that the reason stated in the file might be incomplete or wrong. It is very possible that, when you start investigating, you will find other reasons. A child that has been given up officially because she was 'born from rape' may well discover that her mother was not raped at all, but had to give this reason because if she had told that it was an extramarital child she and her baby would have been expelled by the family. She might even have started a family with the father in question. Always be aware that the adoption history and the reasons for adoption can turn out to be different from what the file says.

Searching for information

If your teenager is looking for information about her history, the best thing you can do is to help her. Talk about the possibilities. Try to make a plan together. Contact the orphanage, foster family, family members, local hospital, doctors, the local police or child protection centre. Ask your teenager what it is she would like to know, what she doesn't want to know. Prepare her for the fact that the information stated in the file could be wrong. This can turn out positively or negatively, but it is important that you are both prepared. Sometimes children find out more by contacting children who are from the same home. Lijnie Siti Slamet (age 28) writes:

> I was looking for similarities in country and heritage. Through the internet I came across Asalsaya, the association for adopted Indonesians. Not that I am ever very active, but it was nice to be able to meet and talk with people of your own age about whatever it is that is bothering you about your adoption, what your views are about adoption programmes on television, or how you feel when others talk about your adoption.[.....] One meeting they arranged was for people who were adopted from the same orphanage. At first I did not even realise that I had stayed in this orphanage in Jakarta before coming to the Netherlands. But after a long investigation through stacks of adoption papers, some names turned up: Kasih Bunda (from the orphanage) and Jane Tumewu (contact person). To me this contact with other Indonesian adopted children felt really good. There is a real sense of a shared background and the others can fill in the gaps in my knowledge. That way the puzzle becomes more and more complete.
> (in Hoksbergen, 2006, p.104)

It may also be possible for you to find more information through specific email or web groups. On the internet there are several orphanage- or birth-country oriented email groups for adoptive parents. It is important that you communicate openly about this with your teenager and that she does not object to your searching in this way.

If your child has a traumatic adoption history, it is especially important that you find as many facts about the past as possible. Perhaps you will be able to discover one or more positive facts or experiences, so your teenager will be able to positively connect to her past in some way. Perhaps there is a story concerning a sweet grandmother or aunt, or someone who has a positive recollection of the time the birth parents had with their child.

Making room for the birth country
It is very important for adopted children to integrate both identities. Therefore, they naturally need to connect with the adoption country as well as the birth country. Try, however, to never force anything onto your teenager; just follow her development. There will probably be periods when she is more or less interested in identifying with her ethnic and cultural background. Possibly there will also be periods when she wants to reject the country of birth.

If there is little or no information available about the birth situation and the adoption, it can be especially important to give attention to your teenager's birth country, so she will at least be able to connect positively with her original culture and ethnic background.

Making room for the birth parents
If you know who the birth parents are, it is important that you help your teenager give them a healthy place in her existence. It doesn't mean that you and your teenager have to meet the birth parents (most teenagers aren't even ready for that), but that you make her parents "visible" in other ways. For example, if you have names

and/or pictures of the parents, you should give them to your child (if you have not done so yet). Let her hang those pictures above her bed if she wants to. Your teenager will be able to connect with her roots naturally, something that will benefit her in developing her identity.

If you know only negative stories about the birth parents, it is important that you search together for positive sides to the history. Your child has undoubtedly received nice things from her family – for example, a talent, her character, the way she carries herself, her eyes, her passion. If your teenager is able to be proud of her heritage, she will develop a more positive identity. Chris da Silva (age 28), after his first meeting with his birth family in Brazil, writes:

> That first time in Brazil, I met a lot of relatives. To my surprise, they were all rather well off. Everyone had a job. One was a baker, the other owned a shoe store, another owned a little bar. Except my nineteen year old sister. My parents and other sisters really pampered her. She was a real beauty. I was so proud of my family. Finally, after all those years, I could be proud of myself. I had the feeling that all the question marks had been erased and that all my questions had been answered. I was someone again. I belonged somewhere.
> (in Hoksbergen, 2006, p.162)

Making memories visible

Every adopted child has pictures, albums, books, belongings, adoption papers, passports or clothing that represent several aspects of the adoption story. If the cherished and important memories stay visible, adopted children are better able to talk about the past. Deborah, in the Dutch NCRV-documentary *Zes Adopties* [Six Adoptions], starts talking immediately when she sees a picture of the past, when she and her sister Andrea were not adopted yet. Even though they fight a lot now, she has always felt a strong connection to her sister:

> I look at that picture, because I sometimes miss the
> [memories]. I get that more and more these days. [...]
> Now sometimes when I look at that picture, I think,
> 'Maybe if I look at it a lot, I will remember more.' Of
> course I love this picture. It is very important to me.
> [She cries.] That picture was taken in 1997, but I can't
> remember it being taken, that is exactly what I regret
> about it. Maybe I repressed it or something... I don't
> know. I would very much like to remember. I wish I
> could go back to where I was then, to look: do I really
> remember? Just to be able to give it a place in my
> memories. [...] I have been thinking about things a lot,
> for a while now. The fact that I cannot remember
> anything, that I know so little. What my parents were
> like, what they look like. I can remember holding her in
> my arms [points at Andrea]. [Silence] That really does a
> lot to me. I remember caring for her when my parents
> were ill. She is almost my baby, that's a strange feeling.

If you feel that your child is thinking about her adoption a lot, you
should ask her questions relating to tangible memories: 'What do
you remember best about your birth country? Which ones do you
like best of those memories? Which ones are hard for you? Which
ones suit you best? Are there things that hurt you or make you
angry? Why?'

Making questions tangible

Feelings and thoughts can be made tangible by writing them down.
It can be very illuminating for a teenager to write down all the
unanswered questions about her adoption. If children can dig up
questions and possible answers, they are better able to understand
that their sadness and anger has a cause, but that it doesn't really
work if you let your whole life be led by these thoughts:

> I felt so relieved when I was allowed to write down
> all the questions without having to find answers or

solutions immediately. I became stronger just by doing it. When I saw that long list of questions, I suddenly understood why I was so on edge sometimes. I also started realising that, by writing all those questions down, you are not immediately looking for an answer to each and every one. There will always be unanswered questions. Maybe someday I will find all the answers, maybe not. Maybe that just wasn't all that important.

Creating space

Although many adopted children deal with their heritage in some way during puberty, there is a chance that your child has been so involved with ordinary adolescent things that the questions about her heritage have been completely suspended or have become unconscious. It is important that you give your child space for this. You may sometimes (when there is a reason) wish to try to ask her something, but keep those questions in tune with the developmental phase your child is in. Keep the subject of her adoption quiet if she is not yet ready for it.

Daring to ask for help

It is never too late to bring in a support worker or to try the sensitive and responsive educational method. Older teenagers can be helped greatly by such a new approach, although in the beginning it may not seem like it.

I had really given up all hope. My 15-year-old daughter was extremely rebellious. She really did not want to see another shrink. Luckily we maintained and visited an adoption support worker together. As a result, our daughter has really changed a lot these last couple of months. She knows her limits now, knows where they come from. She is really very creative in helping to find solutions. A year and a half ago, there was only one thing bothering her: us! Now she asks for help whenever she needs it, and we have had a lot of beautiful conversations since.

Conclusion: taking responsibility

In this chapter, I have given you some tools that can help you to talk about your teenager's adoption history. In earlier chapters I have discussed how to handle automatic thoughts and adoption-related grief. I have shown you how negative basic thoughts can lead to unhealthy grieving emotions like shame, fury and depression. All this information might have given you the idea that an adopted teenager's life is hard and miserable, and that it will be a hard time for the parents and child to work through. However, this does not have to be the case. Adopted children all grieve in different ways and mostly not all of the time. Your teenager will also have a lot of other things to deal with now than just her adoption. The amount of time spent thinking about the adoption will vary greatly from time to time. That she had a bad start in life cannot be doubted. It is important that you validate her pain about this. You can also make her aware that negative feelings and thoughts are not a permanent fact, but that they can be changed into more realistic and productive feelings and thoughts if she wants that to happen. At the same time, however, her own responsibility begins here, because in the end she will have to learn to deal with it herself. Renée Claassen (age 28), writes:

> With everyone who reads this, I would like to share the core of my experience: life is what you make of it. That is just as true for adopted children as for children who weren't adopted. The core is honesty towards yourself, in a healthy way. Do not deny your feelings and do not turn them into an all powerful drama of feelings about adoption. Learning to deal with adoption is a question of meaning, a negative view is self-fulfilling, but the good news is, this is also true for a positive perception. (in Hoksbergen, 2006, p.91, my translation)

Bibliography

Bogaerts, Stefan and van Aelst Gilbert (1998) *Adolescentie en Interculturele adoptie, psychosociale integratie in Vlaamse gezinnen*, Leuven-Apeldoorn: Garant

Brodzinsky, Anne Braff (1996) *The Mulberry Bird: An adoption story*, Indianapolis, IN: Perspectives Press

Brodzinsky, David M (1992) *Being Adopted: The life long search for self*, New York, NY, Double Day

Cohen, Shari (1988) *Coping with Being Adopted*, New York, NY: the Rosen Publishing Group

Delfos, Martine F (2005a) *Ik heb ook wat te vertellen*, Amsterdam: SWP

Delfos, Martine F (2005b) *Ontwikkeling in vogelvlucht*, Amsterdam: Harcourt

Gooden, Janet (2003a) *Informatie bestemd voor ouders over vroege puberteit bij geadopteerde jongens*, Haarlem: Basic Trust

Gooden, Janet (2003b) *Informatie bestemd voor ouders over vroege puberteit bij geadopteerde meisjes*, Haarlem: Basic Trust

Gorbett, Deana (2004) *Adopted Teens Only*, Lincoln: iUniverse

Hasselt-Mooy, Hanneke van (2002) *Huilen, boos zijn, ruzie*, Amsterdam: SWP

Heffels, Annette (2006) *Praten met je puber*, Utrecht: Spectrum

Hoekema, Edy (2002) *Verlies en rouw door adoptie*, Utrecht: SAV

Hoksbergen, René (ed.) (2006) *Vertraagde start, geadopteerden aan het woord*, Soesterberg: Aspekt

Hoksbergen, René and Hans Walenkamp (2000) *Adoptie: een levenslang dilemma*, Houten/Diegem: Bohn Stafleu van Loghum

Juffer, Femmie (1999) *Adoptiekinderen, opvoeding en gehechtheid in het gezin*, Amsterdam: Boom

Keefer, Betsy and Jayne E Schooler (2000) *Telling the Truth to your Adopted or Foster Child*, Westport/Connecticut/London: Bergin en Garvey

Kincher, Jonni (2007) *Ontdek wie je bent, psychologie voor kinderen*, Amsterdam: Nino, SWP

Krementz, Jill (2003) *How it Feels to be Adopted*, New York, NY: Alfred A. Knopf

Melina, Lois Ruskai (2001) *Making Sense of Adoption: A parent's guide*, New York, NY: Harper Collins Publishers

Nijdam, Ronald J (1999) *Adoptees Come of Age*, Louisville, KY: Westminster John Knox Press

Nijmanting, Marieke (2007) *Handboek kindercounseling*, Amsterdam: SWP

Parton, Nigel and O'Byrne, Patrick (2000) *Constructive Social Work: Towards a new practice*, New York, NY: Palgrave. Dutch translated title: *Social Work, een constructieve benadering*, Houten: Bohn Stafleu van Loghum (2007), m.m.v. Carol van Nijnatten.

Polderman, Nelleke (1998) 'Hechtingsstoornis, beginnen bij het begin'. In: *'Tijdschrift voor Orthopedagogiek'*, nummer 10

Polderman, Nelleke (2004) *Toelichting op enkele interactieprincipes van de VIB 12-18 jaar*, versie 2004/1, Haarlem: Basic Trust

Polderman, Nelleke (2006) *Handvatten bij de hulpverlening aan pubers en hun gezinnen*, Haarlem: Basic Trust

Post van der Molen, Daniëlle (2001) *Loyaliteiten gekleurd door adoptie*, Utrecht: SAV

Post van der Molen, Daniëlle and Waller, Marian (2001) *Adoptiekinderen in de puberteit*, Utrecht: SAV

Postema-Velders, Carolien and Loes Sibbing-Willems (2002) *Boosheid en agressie gekleurd door adoptie*, Utrecht: SAV

Riley, Debbie M S, with John Meeks, M D (2005) *Beneath the Mask: Understanding adopted teens*, Silver Spring, MD: CASE

Sitskoorn, Margriet, (2006) *Het maakbare brein*, Amsterdam: Bert Bakker

Starre, Paula (2001) *Zelfbeeld en identiteit gekleurd door adoptie*, Utrecht: SAV

Van den Eerenbeemt, Else-Marie (2003) *De Liefdesladder, over familie en nieuwe liefdes*, Amsterdam-Antwerpen: Archipel

Van den Eerenbeemt, Else-Marie and Ammy van Heusden (2005) *Balans in beweging*, Haarlem: De Toorts

Van Gulden, Holly and Bartels-Rabb, Lisa M (2001) *Real Parents, Real Children*, New York, NY: Crossroad

Van IJzendoorn M H (1994) *Gehechtheid van ouders en kinderen. Intergenerationele overdracht van gehechtheid in theorie (klinisch) onderzoek en gevalsbeschrijvingen*, Bohn Stafl eu Van Loghum

Van IJzendoorn M H and Juffer F (2006) 'The Emanuel Miller Memorial Lecture 2006: Adoption as intervention. Meta-analytic evidence for massive catch-up and plasticity in physical, socio-emotional, and cognitive development', *Journal of Child Psychology*, 47:12, pp.1228–45

Verhulst, Jan (2005) *RET-jezelf*, Amsterdam: Harcourt

Waanders, Liliane (2002) *Op zoek naar je wortels*, Utrecht: SAV

Wolfs, Renée (2008) *Adoption Conversations: What, when and how to tell*, London: BAAF. Translated from Dutch. Original title: *Wereldkind, praten met je adoptiekind*, Amsterdam: De Prom (2004)

Appendix

Principles of Video Interaction Guidance
(from H. Biemans)

Prepared by Nelleke Polderman, Basic Trust, Haarlem, The Netherlands
Translated By Arnoud Visser and Hilary Kennedy, Cupar, Fife, Scotland

 INITIATIVE or ACTION by the child
(words/verbal or behaviour, feeling, wish, thought)

 RECEPTION (confirmation) by the parent/educator

Step 1 | without words: | (friendly) intonation
turning to
eye contact
(friendly) expression
nodding
tone/sound of the
voice attuned

And:

> with words:

- **CONFIRMATION OF RECEIPT** (repetition of what has been said / verbal initiative)

or

- **NAMING** (identifying) of behaviour, feelings, wishes, thoughts, intentions.

 INITIATIVE of the educator/parent:

Step 2 give opinion
make yourself explicit
make a circle (divide turns)
study in depth
chatter
make a suggestion
name oppositions
positive prompting (offering a structure)
paying a compliment

Step 3 **(especially important in talking with teenangers)**
possibly after giving an opinion or making a suggestion:

Ask for a confirmation of receipt

or

Ask for a reaction to what has been said

INITIATIVE or (RE)ACTION of child, etc.